W9-BTE-587

EDUCATiON
LiBRARY

QUEEN'S UNiVERSiTY
AT KiNGSTON

KiNGSTON   ONTARiO   CANADA

MAKING YOUR OWN
NATURE MUSEUM

MAKING YOUR OWN NATURE MUSEUM

BY RUTH B. (ALFORD)
MacFARLANE

ILLUSTRATED BY
JEAN LYNN ALRED

Franklin Watts
New York / London / Toronto / Sydney
A Venture Book / 1989

ʃᴜᴜᴠ   QH 70. AIM3   1989

Photographs courtesy of
Dan Urbanski: 11, 42, 70; Rick
McKay: 39 (both); Robert Aho: 45; Owen Alford: 65.

Library of Congress Cataloging-in-Publication Data
MacFarlane, Ruth B. Alford.
Making your own nature museum / Ruth B. (Alford) MacFarlane :
illustrated by Jean Lynn Alred.
p.   cm.—(A Venture book)
Summary: Gives instructions for collecting, preserving,
identifying, and displaying a nature collection.
ISBN 0-531-10809-0
1. Natural history—Exhibitions—Design and construction—Juvenile
literature.   2. Biological specimens—Collection and preservation—
Juvenile literature.   3. Geological specimens—Collection and
preservation—Juvenile literature.   4. Natural history museums—
Juvenile literature.   [1. Natural history—Exhibitions—Design and
construction   2. Biological specimens—Collection and preservation.
3. Geological specimens—Collection and preservation.]   I. Alred,
Jean Lynn, ill.   II. Title.
QH70.AIM3   1989
508'.075'3—dc20   89-31826   CIP   AC

Copyright © 1989 by Ruth B. (Alford) MacFarlane
All rights reserved
Printed in the United States of America
6   5   4   3   2   1

CONTENTS

MAKING YOUR OWN
NATURE MUSEUM

ONE

MAKING A
NATURE MUSEUM

Perhaps you want to do something with the rocks, leaves, feathers, and shells you are always bringing home. Or maybe you need to do a science project for school, a science fair, summer camp, Scouts, or 4-H club. Arranging your natural specimens into a display or project or collecting new specimens for a specific project may be just the solution.

Although you may not think of such collections as a nature museum, in fact they are. True, the typical nature museum may be a whole building overflowing with stuffed owls, rock collections, glass cabinets lined with thousands of insects, and so on. But you can think of your science project display as a small nature museum, just as you can think of a specimen-covered bookshelf in your bedroom, a classroom display cabinet, or elaborate basement display as a nature museum.

Probably the main requirement of your display, collection, or museum—it doesn't matter what you call it—is that it should do what you want it to. A shelf in your bedroom may be fine for odds and ends, but a more elaborate setup might be needed to adequately display specimens for a classroom or science fair project.

Whatever kind of nature display you put together, you will want to be creative and to arrange your display attractively and meaningfully. That could mean putting all the rocks in one place and all the shells in another, or it could mean carefully labeling every specimen, preparing cards telling where you found them, and displaying only those specimens that tell a particular story or that prove some point.

Although professional nature museums usually contain stuffed animals, the emphasis in this book is on not killing. Human beings share the earth with other creatures and living organisms, so we shouldn't have to destroy life to appreciate and learn from it.

Animals leave footprints, birds drop feathers, trees drop acorns, shellfish die and leave their shells behind. You can collect some of these things without harming anything. You can also take pictures or make drawings instead of collecting actual specimens. In fact, if you become a detective looking for clues left by your feathered or furred friends, you will have plenty of objects to gather for your collection.

This book will show you how to collect and preserve specimens, how to build displays, and how to turn your displays into a project you can use for fun or to fulfill an assignment. You can collect first and build

*A one-shelf home collection (top) and (below)
an elaborate collection built on one bedroom wall*

your display later, or set up the space first and then fill it. If you do the latter, just start this book with Chapter 9.

You may do only one project, or you may build a whole museum in your garage. Start simply, but practice each technique and do it as well as you can. At first you will probably feel slow and clumsy, but you will gain speed and competence. You may become inspired to go on and study to be a naturalist or other scientist, one day joining the staff of a nature museum, or perhaps even going on research expeditions sponsored by universities or the National Geographic Society.

TWO

THE ART OF COLLECTING

Whatever your reason for collecting specimens, you will need to know *how* to collect them. If you are basically a random collector who wants to put together a loose display of specimens, you can learn a few techniques here that will make collecting more fun. If, on the other hand, you are following specific guidelines such as those often established for science-fair or county-fair projects, the methods and ideas presented here will help ensure that you don't get disqualified or don't lose because you were careless.

YOUR PLAN OF ACTION

A scientist doesn't just pick up a rock here, a shell there, or a handful of flowers across the road. A scientist collects with a purpose. As a beginner, you may collect at random, but if you are doing a formal science project, you will need to have a very specific purpose.

A simple plan might be: "Collect rocks." This sort of plan probably would not win you a science-fair medal, but it would be fun to do. A more detailed plan might be: "Collect abandoned wasps' nests. Note where they are found and whether any wasps are nearby. Collect some of the wasps. Photograph the area and describe the soil, trees, and other vegetation. Find out the factors in the habitat that affect wasp populations."

A general plan is: "Collect different specimens from the school (or camp) grounds: plants, insects, rocks, soil, and traces of animals and birds."

More specific plans are: "Collect samples of different soil types in my county and then do some research on soil formation," or, "Collect the leaves, flowers, fruits, and bark of all the maples in my county." A still more involved plan might be: "Collect the stages in the life cycle of the cabbage butterfly."

For a science-fair project, you may want to do original research and follow formal methods of experimentation. Suppose that you have a hunch or theory as to why one kind of moth is more common than another in the nearby park. To prove or disprove your theory, you would need to identify, photograph or collect (with permission) both moths and plants; watch for possible insect, bird, or animal enemies; and record the weather, sources of pollution, and use of sprays. A display adds visual impact to your written report. More information on this type of project can be found in some of the books on science-fair projects listed in the Bibliography at the back of this book.

Your plan will depend on your interests, on your assignment or aims, and on what is available. There may be a lot of fossils near you, or perhaps there is a nearby beach that has shells and skeletons of sea creatures and beautiful sea plants. If you live in the country, you can search the fields, woods, and streams for a great variety of plants or animals, but even in the city you can find a surprising number of wild creatures and plants. If you take a trip, of course, there will be new opportunities for collecting. You might plan a project around such a trip.

TOOLS, SUPPLIES, AND CLOTHING

When you go out collecting, you will need certain tools and supplies. Take a backpack or knapsack containing all or some of the following: a digging implement such as a trowel, tags or adhesive tape for labeling specimens, plastic food-storage bags, small plastic containers, a metric ruler, a magnifying glass or hand lens, and a pocket knife. If you are doing a specific type of collecting, for example, looking for fossils, you will need special tools. You may also need a camera, film, plaster of paris, or a sketch pad.

Always carry a small notebook (which you can hang by a string from your neck) and a pencil (ink runs), so that you can take notes.

Dress comfortably, take insect repellent and suntan

lotion, and carry food and water. Also take along work gloves and a hat. If you are going to be in heavy brush or boggy ground or any other special conditions, wear heavy jeans, hiking boots, or other special clothing. A map and compass and field guides may be appropriate.

Practice collecting close to home until you gain confidence. At first you may make some mistakes or forget to take along needed equipment.

KEEPING RECORDS

You will want to record information in your field notebook right when you collect a specimen. Keeping field notes will make the difference between having just an interesting object to look at and a scientific specimen. Tell where and when you found it. "Where" is the state, county, parish, township, city, etc. "When" is the day, month, and year, usually written in that order: "26 September 1989."

Include other information such as color, odor, and surrounding conditions. Did the flower smell like a skunk? Was the bone half buried in garden soil? Was the fungus growing on a dead tree? If you are taking pictures or making drawings, you may have additional notes: "The grouse was one of ten," or "Footprints were 25 cm apart."

Number your specimen immediately. The first specimen you collect will be No. 1; the second, No. 2, and so on. Write that number in your notebook and put it on your specimen, using a small tag, adhesive tape, or a piece of paper placed with the specimen. See Figure 1.

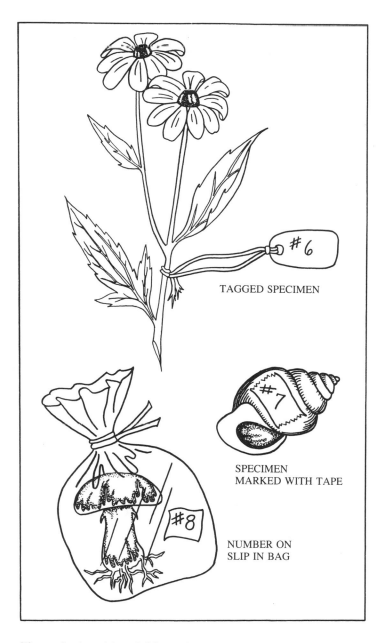

TAGGED SPECIMEN

SPECIMEN
MARKED WITH TAPE

NUMBER ON
SLIP IN BAG

Figure 1. Attaching field numbers

A sample entry in your field notebook might be: "No. 1. 26 September 1989. Michigan, Ontonagon County, Greenland Township. Skull found under oak tree in farm field along Rousseau Rd. 3 miles southeast of Mass City. Lying on top of clay ground but under dead leaves. Very white. No other bones nearby."

Field notes such as these enable a scientist to make an identification back in the lab or to know what the specimen is long after it was collected. If you take pictures, be sure to keep a record of each.

When you leave "the field," write the field number on the envelope, coffee can, or other container in which you are storing your specimen.

METHODS OF COLLECTING

You can collect an actual organism, like a plant or insect, or you can collect the *traces* left behind by organisms, such as feathers, bones, abandoned nests, skins of snakes and insects, footprints, and seeds.

You can also take photographs or make drawings.

Photographs

When you take a photograph, focus on important characteristics, because outdoor nature shots can be uninformative if not set up properly. You may want to photograph plants, rocks, and other stationary objects or organisms against a background, for example, sturdy cardboard (2 × 3 ft. or 60 × 90 cm).

Experiment with contrasting colors, with black, and with white, which will brighten the photo. Be sure to include a ruler in your photo if you can, to show size. In your notebook, record the same information you would if you were collecting an actual specimen.

Drawings
A drawing can emphasize details that may be hard to show in a photograph. In addition, the process of drawing helps you to observe more closely than you might if you just picked up something. You might want to catch a spectacular beetle or moth, keep it for a while in a clear container, draw it, then release it.

Making Rubbings
You can do rubbings to capture outlines and textures of plant specimens. Lay a sheet of white paper against the bark of a tree and rub the side of a dark crayon over the paper. Also try making rubbings of leaves. Is there anything else on which the rubbing technique might work?

ETIQUETTE AND ETHICS

When you are in the field, try to disturb as few things as possible. If you are collecting wildflowers, you need not pick more than a couple. If you see only one example of a specimen, leave it and move on to something else. If you are collecting fossils, don't take them all. Avoid crushing plants or breaking branches when you walk; don't throw things or make loud noises, and be sure to replace stones you may lift to observe the life under them. If you pick up a shell and find a creature in the shell, put it back. In other words, walk softly.

Don't trespass on private property without obtaining permission from the owners, and don't collect in places where it is forbidden. Most state and national parks prohibit collecting, and you can't collect in the tidepools of California, however many little crabs you see scurrying around the rocks. If you are careful and courteous, property owners and park rangers may actually help you with your project.

Be sure not to take any protected or endangered species. Lists of such plants and animals are available from your library, science teacher, and other sources. If you find something you think is rare, report it to the nearest college biology department or to a natural history museum.

IDENTIFYING SPECIMENS

What kind of flower did you find? Do you have a piece of jade or just a plain green stone? What creature left that shell? Once you find a specimen or traces of some beast (for example, tracks), you will want to know what you have found. Some organisms are easy to identify in the field, using a field guide. Others must be brought back to your home or school and dissected or examined carefully using a microscope. You can compare your specimens with those found in museums, or you can use a "key," a printed list of choices that will lead you step by step to the correct name. Field guides and other identification books are listed in the Bibliography at the back of this book.

SAFETY

Before you go into the field, check with one of your parents, or with a counselor if you are at camp. If your trip is approved, it is still best to go with a friend—if your parent or counselor isn't going to accompany you.

Watch for poisonous plants like poison ivy, poison oak, and poison sumac, a 9-ft. (3-m) shrub found in boggy places. All of these produce an uncomfortable, itching rash in many people. See Figure 2.

Avoid the discomfort caused by these plants by learning to recognize them, wearing long pants and long-sleeved shirts, and by staying on trails and roads.

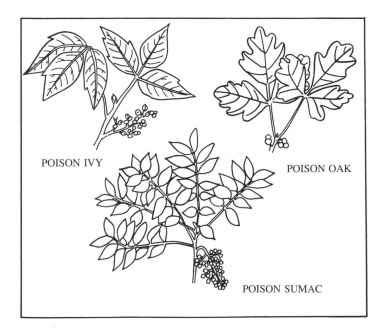

Figure 2. Poisonous plants

Also watch out for poisonous snakes like rattle-snakes and copperheads, or other poisonous creatures likely to be encountered in your area. Learn to recognize them by their appearance and other telltale signs.

RESOURCES

For information on all sorts of natural history questions, write to:

The American Museum of Natural History
Central Park West at 79th Street
New York, NY 10024

National Museum of Natural History
The Smithsonian Institution
1000 Jefferson Drive SW
Washington, DC 20560

United States Department of Agriculture
Independence Avenue
Washington, DC 20250

Your state Department of Natural Resources (or of Conservation) is located in your state capital, and is probably listed in your telephone directory under your state name (for example, "Michigan, State of, Dept. of Natural Resources").

State colleges often maintain extension offices that can provide pamphlets. Look under "(your state) University Cooperative Extension Service" in the telephone directory, or ask your librarian how to find the address.

Consult teachers, Boy and Girl Scout or 4-H leaders, museum curators, and other experts. Visit museums and join groups like the Audubon Society or botanical clubs or rock and mineral societies.

Whenever you write for information, enclose a self-addressed, stamped envelope, to save the other person time and expense. After all, you are the one asking the favor.

Best of all, go to your nearest library. Consult the card catalog, search the shelves, or talk to the librarian. If you don't find exactly the book you need, look for related ones. The librarian may be able to find a particular book for you. Look at both juvenile and adult books. Those for younger readers, often beautifully illustrated, will give you simple beginning explanations and pictures, perhaps all you need for now. Books designed for high-schoolers and adults will lead you on to deeper study. Consult the Bibliography at the back of this book for suggested references.

THREE

COLLECTING AND PRESERVING PLANTS

Plants are among the easiest of nature's offspring to study, incorporate into a project, and display. They are everywhere, so to keep from being overwhelmed by the possibilities, it will be best to have a project in mind and to develop a collecting plan. Two possible projects could be: "Plants found in a vacant city lot," or "Spring flowers from my farm."

Most plants have flowers of one kind or another. These include trees like maples, vines like grape and wild cucumber, and soft-stemmed plants like daisies, violets, and even grasses. Most weeds are flowering plants.

COLLECTING
FLOWERING PLANTS

Look for plants in your own yard, if you have one, or along roadsides and in vacant lots. Go walking in fields and woods and along streams and the shores of lakes and the ocean. Ask gardeners, greenhouse keepers, and farmers to let you have both cultivated plants and weeds.

You can collect, draw, or photograph whole plants or just parts: leaves, flowers, and twigs; cones, nuts, seeds, or other fruits; bark and wood samples; and examples of plant diseases.

If a plant is fairly small, you can collect all of it. Dig it out carefully, shake or wash the dirt from the roots, place it in a plastic bag along with a numbered tag, and seal the top to prevent wilting. Besides telling where and when you found it, tell whether it was growing in sun or shade, in wet or dry soil, and the type of soil: clay, sand, gravel, leafy forest loam, rocks, mud, etc. Record the flower color too, which may fade in drying.

If the plant is large, cut off a piece about 10 in. (25 cm) long, enough to have at least two leaves to help in identification. You will need to be able to see the pattern of leaf growth (pairs of leaves, whorls, etc.). Take a second sample so you have one to preserve and one to identify. In your field notebook describe the rest of the plant, for example: "tall tree, smooth gray bark." Ideally, try to identify it on the spot.

The best plant specimens have flowers or fruits on them as well as leaves, although you may make a collection of leaves or of flowers or of fruits alone. When collecting only parts, record the information about the whole plant.

Bark

You can collect bark in several ways. You can peel pieces of bark from branches or trunks that have been

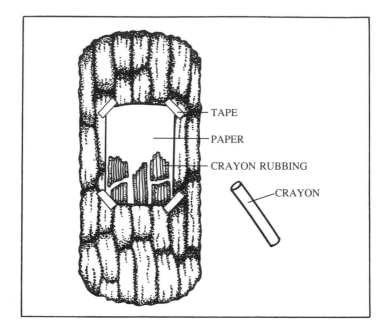

Figure 3. A bark rubbing

cut or have fallen down for some reason, perhaps cut for firewood, but never from a living tree. A piece about 6×8 in. (15×20 cm) would show the basic texture.

You also can make bark rubbings by taping paper over the bark (while still on the tree) and rubbing crayon over the paper. Figure 3 shows an example. You could also photograph or draw the bark. If you stand the same distance from each tree while taking pictures, your photos will show comparative sizes of patterns.

Wood
Wood samples show the grain or interior structure of different trees. You can collect wood in two ways.

Slab-type samples about 2 × 6 in. (5 × 15 cm) can be made from scraps of wood or discarded furniture from lumber yards, your school's woodworking shop, or other similar places. You can also buy wood from stores or special wood-supply companies. Exotic wood from different parts of the world can be bought from some of these companies.

The second way to obtain wood is to collect dead or fallen branches or trimmings. Try to find pieces with undamaged bark, and cut them to a size of about 2 × 10 in. (5 × 25 cm).

Be sure to label all the wood, regardless of how it was obtained. When you collect wood using the second method, record the size of the tree and the shape of the tree and its leaves, and describe any flowers or fruits. Collect cones, leaves, flowers, etc. These will help you to identify the tree.

Plant Galls

Some plants get strange growths called plant galls, which can be studied or made into an interesting collection. Plant galls are formed when an insect lays its eggs in a plant and the plant responds by growing a protective cushion around it (see Figure 4). The wormlike insect larva feeds on the plant, usually without killing it, and eventually emerges as an adult insect.

When collecting galls, try to find one with an insect larva still inside. (When an insect emerges, it leaves a little hole behind in the gall.) To coax out any insects, place the whole plant stalk, gall and all, in a jar of water in an insect-rearing cage and wait. After a while, an insect may emerge. If you save the insect and the

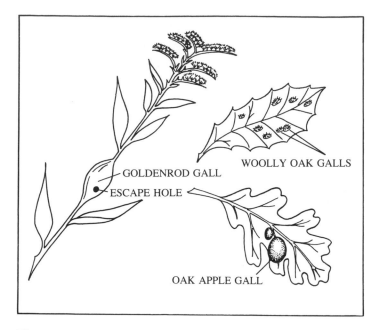

GOLDENROD GALL

ESCAPE HOLE

WOOLLY OAK GALLS

OAK APPLE GALL

Figure 4. Three different types of plant galls

gall, you will have a display that tells a story. A collection of different galls and their insects would make an excellent exhibit.

COLLECTING NON-FLOWERING PLANTS

Ferns and some other plants like horsetails and ground pines have neither flowers nor seeds. Instead they reproduce by spores produced in brownish spots on the backs or edges of the leaves or fronds, or in special conelike structures or stalks. Ferns are beautiful when pressed, but they are quick to wilt. You might have to carry along a plant press and press them right away to get specimens that are not all curled and crumpled. Horsetails, on the other hand, are stiff and easily carried home. Before collecting any ground pines, make sure they are not protected plants in your area.

COLLECTING LICHENS

Lichens (pronounced LI-kens in the United States and LITCH-ens in Great Britain) are interesting structures formed by algae and fungi growing together. Lichens may cover the ground, crackling underfoot, or form circles on tree trunks, or hang wisping down from tree branches. Lichens are often pale green or blue-green, but some are orange, yellow, black, and other bold colors. You should be able to collect and identify some of the larger and more common ones.

While the tiny lichens that grow on rocks are hard to collect (except with a camera and closeup lens), the larger clumps are easy. They actually can be kept alive in your collection by either planting them or simply putting them on some dirt or among some pebbles and occasionally wetting them with a plant-mister.

PRESERVING PLANTS

When you return from a collecting trip, it is best to preserve plants right away. If you cannot, you can store most of them in plastic bags in a refrigerator (not a freezer) for up to 24 hours.

Some plant specimens don't need special treatment

to be preserved, but most do. If you want the plants as part of a three-dimensional exhibit, simply hang them upside down to dry in a warm, dark place like a closet for a few weeks. However, the usual method is to press and dry them.

Plants are normally pressed in a plant press. You can buy a plant press or you can make your own, or you can simply press and dry plants with sheets of newspapers and heavy weights. Whichever way you plan to work, the basic aim and mechanism are the same: to dry and flatten plant parts using blotters or thick paper (to absorb moisture from the plant) and weight (to flatten and preserve the shape of the plant). You may press a whole plant or only its leaves, flowers, or twigs. Small seed pods can also be pressed.

To make your own press (Figure 5), you will need two pieces of ¼-in. plywood or pegboard 12 × 18 in. (30 × 46 cm) for the rigid outside covers and several pieces of cardboard and sheets of blotter paper or folded newspaper the same dimensions. The outside covers can also be made of a grid of wooden strips, each about ¾ in. (2 cm) square, fastened with glue and either nails or screws at each intersection. Figure 5 shows the latter type of cover, while Figure 6F shows the way the covers, cardboard, and paper or blotters are arranged before pressing. The straps you see around the press in Figure 6G are webbing straps with gripper buckles.

To use your plant press,

1. As shown in Figure 6A, fold a single sheet of newspaper in half crosswise. On the outside edge, write your field number and the date the plant was collected.

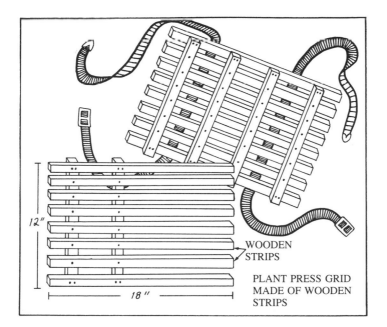

Figure 5. Making a plant press

2. Referring to Figure 6B, spread out the plant inside the single sheet, turning over at least one leaf to show the underside (important in identification). Press some flowers open to show the center. Hold the plant parts in place with strips of wet newspaper about $\frac{3}{4} \times 3$ in. (2×7 cm) or by using little weights (stones or other small, heavy objects).

3. If the plant is too large to fit the paper on which you plan to mount it, fold it sharply into the shape of a V, N, or W, or cut off part of it, as shown in Figure 6C.

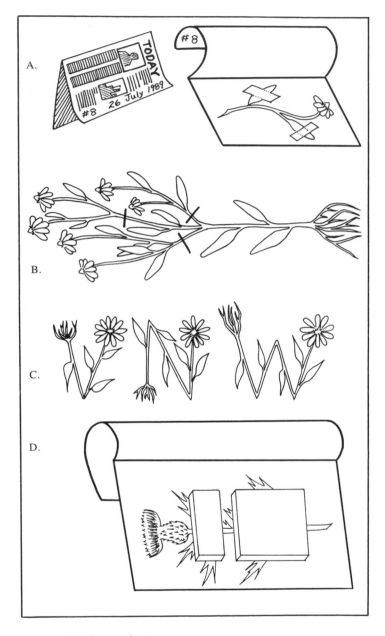

Figure 6. Using a plant press

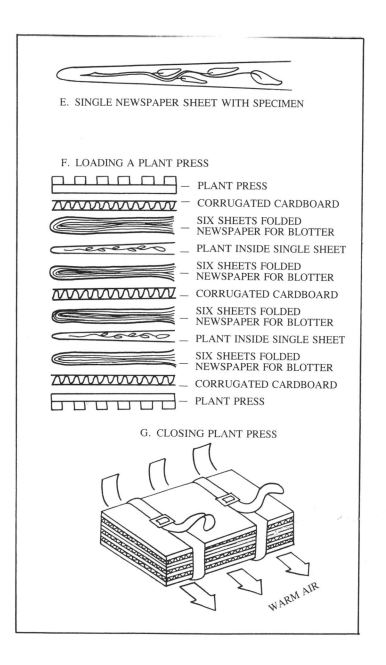

E. SINGLE NEWSPAPER SHEET WITH SPECIMEN

F. LOADING A PLANT PRESS

— PLANT PRESS

— CORRUGATED CARDBOARD

— SIX SHEETS FOLDED NEWSPAPER FOR BLOTTER

— PLANT INSIDE SINGLE SHEET

— SIX SHEETS FOLDED NEWSPAPER FOR BLOTTER

— CORRUGATED CARDBOARD

— SIX SHEETS FOLDED NEWSPAPER FOR BLOTTER

— PLANT INSIDE SINGLE SHEET

— SIX SHEETS FOLDED NEWSPAPER FOR BLOTTER

— CORRUGATED CARDBOARD

— PLANT PRESS

G. CLOSING PLANT PRESS

WARM AIR

4. Figure 6D shows you how to deal with lumpy plants (e.g., twigs). You will need to equalize the pressure of the plant press by placing pads of plastic foam or folded newspaper over the thinner plant parts.

5. Bring the other half of the folded newspaper over the flattened plant, as shown in Figure 6E.

6. Figure 6F shows you the final arrangements before the press is strapped shut. You will be placing the single sheet containing the plant between two blotters or thick pads of newspaper to absorb moisture. Then you will be placing the newspaper-blotter-plant sandwich between two pieces of cardboard and setting the sandwich in the press. Continue pressing plants and placing the sandwiches in the press.

7. Finally, strap the press shut, as shown in Figure 6G. Insufficient tightening results in wrinkled plants.

8. Set the press in a warm place to dry. Quick drying helps to retain color and prevent mold. Outdoors in the sun, in an open window, or on top of a mild heat source is best. An oven is too hot. Be careful you don't start a fire.

9. After 24 hours, remove the blotters, or replace them if the plant is still damp.

10. After about a week, the plants should be thoroughly dry. Take them out of the press, but keep them in their single newspaper sheets and store them in labeled protective folders until you are ready to use them.

Dry Fruits and Bark
Cones, nuts, acorns, seeds, other dry fruits, and bark can be air dried and stored in numbered boxes or envelopes until you are ready to work with them. Some of these plant parts might contain insects that could de-

stroy your collection. Kill these insects by fumigating them for 24 hours with nail-polish remover inside a tightly closed container like a plastic bag.

Fleshy Fruits

Fleshy fruits like apples or plums can be preserved in rubbing alcohol. You might cut the fruit in half to show the placement of the seeds.

Wood

Wood needs only to be dried to preserve it, but to demonstrate the wood grain from different viewpoints, cut the piece of branch as shown in Figure 7. Shellac or varnish one-half of the cut surfaces.

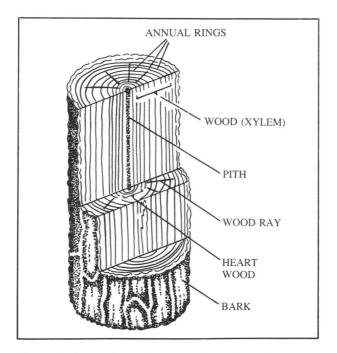

Figure 7. A wood sample cut to show the grain

FOUR

COLLECTING AND PRESERVING ANIMALS: VERTEBRATES

The animal world includes just about everything living that moves (and some things that don't) from polar bears to mosquitoes to clams. Animals with internal skeletons—backbones—are called vertebrates. Mammals, birds, fish, reptiles (like snakes), and amphibians (like frogs) are vertebrates.

A nature collection would probably not seem complete without vertebrate exhibits. These can be as simple as a labeled skull or as complicated as a diorama, an exhibit containing stuffed or model animals in a setting designed to look like the animal's natural habitat.

Collecting animal specimens for a science project or for your own displays can be challenging. Like plants, animals inhabit all kinds of places, from city apartments to dense forests to oceans. Unlike plants, animals are often hard to find, and even when you find them, they usually won't sit still for you either to collect them, or photograph or sketch them. You have to be a bit like a detective gathering clues.

In this chapter you will learn how to "stalk" vertebrate prey and how to collect *without* killing or trapping, and you will be given suggestions for projects.

WHY YOU SHOULD NOT KILL OR TRAP VERTEBRATES

There are a number of reasons you should not kill or trap vertebrates for your collection, and there are still more reasons why you don't have to.

1. Most vertebrates are protected by law. Nongame birds cannot be killed under any circumstances, while a license is required to kill game birds and mammals—assuming hunting them is allowed.

2. Many fish, reptiles, birds, and other vertebrates are becoming scarce or even extinct.

3. Some mammals carry dangerous diseases like rabies or bubonic plague.

4. Many people believe it is wrong to kill animals.

5. Preparing vertebrates for display requires long study and training in taxidermy.

6. Vertebrate projects and exhibits may be prohibited from science fairs.

7. And finally, special regulations, some enforced by the federal government, govern the use of vertebrates in scientific experimentation.

Even collecting flattened fauna—dead animals on the side of a road—requires a special license.

The fact is that literally thousands of projects can be done and collections built without killing a single living creature. Many ideas are given throughout this book; in fact, Chapter 10 consists entirely of ideas. Many of the books in the Bibliography give still more ideas for projects.

PHOTOGRAPHING AND DRAWING VERTEBRATES

The easiest, safest, most humane ways to "collect" animals are to take their pictures or draw them. Imagine snapping a picture of a deer browsing on twigs or wading in a stream, of a pigeon brooding its young on a city ledge, or of a raccoon craftily removing the lid from a garbage can. These sorts of scenes have to be captured on film—there's no other way. Some of the most famous hunters and hunting writers have given up shooting animals with guns in favor of shooting them with cameras. Their photographs can often be found in such magazines as *Outdoor Life* and *Field and Stream*.

You can also sketch animals. Sketching will help you observe more carefully and will enable you to emphasize things about an animal even a camera will not pick up. You could mix photos and drawings in a display, perhaps filling in the blanks in a photo essay with drawings of your own creation but based on research.

Many books on nature photography and drawing have been published. A few are listed in the Bibliography at the back of this book. Photography and drawing can be used in all the following sections on collecting, observing, and preserving animal parts and signs of animal activity.

*Photos of
animals
taken by
a youth
during
a trip
to North
Dakota*

COLLECTING BONES
AND OTHER
ANIMAL PARTS

Collecting bones, skulls, horns, claws, fur, and teeth is a good way to learn some anatomy and to gather objects for your nature museum. Unless you can identify an animal from its parts, you probably will have to do some research to figure out what it is. You can start your research with Figure 8, which shows the skeleton of a cat. Most mammals are put together in somewhat the same way.

When you come across animal parts, photograph or sketch them exactly the way they are lying so that you can reassemble them later in the correct order. Note any signs of a struggle if the bones seem fresh—for example, feathers or pieces of fur scattered about.

Use a grasping instrument like tongs to carefully gather up every last bone, tooth, or other part you find. Wrap each in numbered paper. **Since the bones of some animals may carry disease, do not touch the bones directly. Avoid bones that are too fresh.** The best ones are whitened with age—hard and dry. Record field notes on your find.

You can also use bones from meat products served in your home or in restaurants. Butchers often have unusual bones such as oxtails or animal parts like chicken feet. If anyone in your family hunts, you will be able to obtain the inedible parts of game—antlers, claws, horns, bones, teeth, feathers, and scales. You could, for example, make a project using the skeleton of a rabbit or deer.

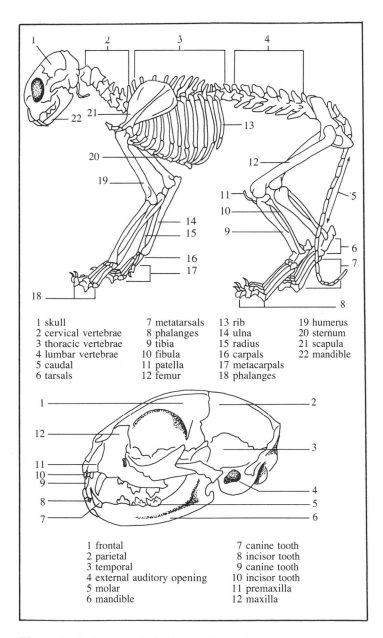

1 skull	7 metatarsals	13 rib	19 humerus
2 cervical vertebrae	8 phalanges	14 ulna	20 sternum
3 thoracic vertebrae	9 tibia	15 radius	21 scapula
4 lumbar vertebrae	10 fibula	16 carpals	22 mandible
5 caudal	11 patella	17 metacarpals	
6 tarsals	12 femur	18 phalanges	

1 frontal	7 canine tooth
2 parietal	8 incisor tooth
3 temporal	9 canine tooth
4 external auditory opening	10 incisor tooth
5 molar	11 premaxilla
6 mandible	12 maxilla

Figure 8. Skeleton and skull of a domestic cat

Sorting the bones of a coyote skeleton

Other possibilities are snake skins shed as a snake grows and skeletons of fish or frogs cleaned by birds.

COLLECTING
ANIMAL TRACKS

A good naturalist can identify an animal by the tracks it leaves. You can "collect" tracks by making casts of them (see page 49) or by drawing or photographing them.

The best place to find tracks is in mud, wet sand, or snow. If you have ever camped near a stream, you may have seen tracks that looked like little handprints. They probably were made by a raccoon. You can also prepare a special bed for animal tracks by clearing away debris and smoothing a patch of mud or wet sand in a place visited by birds or other animals. Many field guides contain drawings of tracks to help you identify the animals that made them.

COLLECTING
BIRD PELLETS

Owls and hawks and some other birds of prey spit up pellets containing their prey's indigestible hair, small bones, and teeth. They are usually dry and won't offend your sense of smell or squeamishness. Look for pellets at the base of trees and other perching places. Watch and listen to learn the kind of owl or hawk that frequents the spot. You can also buy pellets from mail-order science and nature companies. You can combine pellets with other parts of a display, but by themselves they make interesting exhibits. If you study them, you can tell what the birds that left them were eating.

COLLECTING AND OBSERVING OTHER SIGNS OF ANIMAL ACTIVITY

Animals leave other signs of their presence.

• Beavers gnaw trees, leaving a telltale trunk, wood chips, and other signs. Beavers also build dams, and although spotting beavers is difficult (the best time is dusk), finding beaver dams and lodges is not. If you live near a marshy area, there is a good chance you will come across a beaver dam. You can put together an interesting display by exhibiting chips and gnawed wood along with photographs of a lodge and the surrounding pond. You can then provide extensive notes describing what happens when a beaver or beavers work over an area.

• Birds and small animals leave nests. You can collect nests in fall after the birds have gone away or when the animals are done with them. Never disturb an active bird's nest or take eggs. You can, however, pick up eggshells after the young have hatched. If you have a telephoto lens, you could photograph the activity around a nest being used.

• Burrows—animal holes—can be photographed or drawn. Some people put luminescent powder near burrows so they can track the nighttime activity of the animal inhabitants. The animals leave glowing tracks that can be followed.

Beaver dam, lodge, and pond

• You can collect feathers and try to identify them.

• Animals leave traces of their feeding activity—small shrubs neatly nipped off at an angle by rabbits, young apple trees with the bark stripped away by rabbits or maybe deer, acorns or nuts gnawed by squirrels, piles of pinecone tailings left by a squirrel or chipmunk, a little pile of cut-off grass pieces stored by a meadow mouse, millet seeds discarded by chickadees, and so on. See Figure 9. Study a field guide to animal tracks for more ideas.

• Birds and other animals make sounds that can be tape-recorded using a portable machine. You can describe the bird or identify it before or after the sound

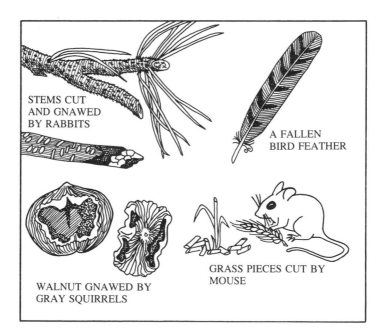

Figure 9. Traces of animal activity

itself—on tape! Answer questions such as: Is it as big as a sparrow, robin, or crow? What kind of bill does it have—slender and small, heavy, long, curved, or straight? What colors are the back, breast, belly, tail, and head? Does the bird have any special markings, such as bars on the wings, a band on the tail, or a ring around the eye? Describe the bird's behavior: Is it fluttering its wings, pecking other birds, gathering grass stems? You can play the tape when visitors view your exhibits.

WORKING WITH PETS

Pets are animals too. They leave traces of their activity that you can collect, and they exhibit behaviors you can study and capture on film or in drawings.

For example: Dogs can have fleas, they eat in a distinctive manner, they shed, they need their toenails clipped, and they leave footprints (sometimes on the kitchen floor). If you imagine your pet as a wild animal, there are plenty of things you can collect for an exhibit or project.

Photograph your pet's natural behavior (not the tricks you have taught it)—eating, circling, digging, or hunting. If your cat goes outdoors, you can watch it stalk a bird. How do your gerbils react to changes in the weather? There are hundreds of possibilities.

LABELING AND
IDENTIFYING SPECIMENS

Be sure to label specimens in the field. Identify them using standard field guides to mammals, fish, animal tracks, birds, and so forth.

PRESERVING
BONES, TRACKS,
AND OTHER TRACES

You will need to preserve your specimens and tracks so that you can display them later.

Bones, Skulls, and Teeth
Fumigate objects found in the wild to rid them of insects. Place them, along with a few cotton balls soaked in nail-polish remover, in a tightly closed plastic bag for 24 hours. Then clean the objects by washing them or brushing them gently.

For parts of animals obtained from hunters or stores, boil them gently in water, remove the meat from the bones, then soak in liquid bleach mixed with water (one part bleach to one part water). **Be careful not to get bleach on your skin or in your eyes. Work in a well-ventilated room.** Leave the bones in the bleach solution for 15 minutes, rinse them in clear water, and check to see what progress has been made. Soak them longer if necessary. Clean the bones by brushing them and picking off the remaining meat with tweezers or forceps. It is important to remove every last bit of flesh, or the meat will rot and create a stench. Big, heavy bones will take more soaking than small ones.

Wash your hands, utensils, and work area with plenty of soap and hot water when you are through.

If you find the preparation of skeletons especially interesting, try to obtain a copy of the book, *Anatomical Preparations,* listed in the Bibliography.

Store these objects in labeled boxes until you are ready to display them.

Animal Tracks

To preserve animal tracks, make a cast in the field. You will need a strip of cardboard, water, plaster of paris, and a flat stick for stirring. Bend the strip of cardboard into a circle larger than the track. Clear away any twigs or debris. Press the cardboard into the dirt, encircling the footprint.

Add about ¼ cup (60 ml) of plaster of paris to an equal amount of water, stir with a flat stick until smooth (it should be about like thick cream or a milkshake), and pour the mixture into the print. Let the mixture harden 30 minutes and carefully lift it up. You will have a cast of a footprint. Number it as a specimen and record all necessary data in your field notebook. See Figure 10.

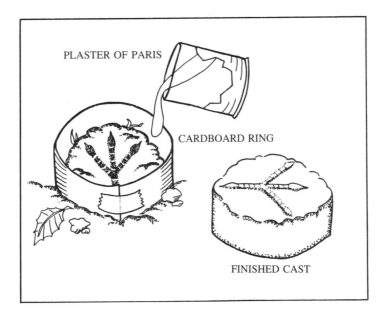

PLASTER OF PARIS

CARDBOARD RING

FINISHED CAST

Figure 10. Making a cast of animal tracks

Skin and Fur

Special methods may be required to preserve these animal parts. Look for a book on taxidermy and ask for help from an experienced adult if you want to do much work with skins and hides. When you store these objects, be sure to protect them from insect damage by packing them in bags with mothballs, or display them in tightly closed cases.

Now that you have learned how to work with vertebrates, it is time to move on to invertebrates.

FIVE

COLLECTING AND PRESERVING ANIMALS: INVERTEBRATES

Invertebrates are animals without backbones. Some invertebrates, such as insects, spiders, crabs, and crayfish, have hard outer coverings called exoskeletons. Others make shells for themselves, for example, snails, clams, oysters, and barnacles. Some are soft-bodied, with no skeletons at all, like worms and leeches. Invertebrates generally tend to be smaller than vertebrates, although there are some notable exceptions, for example, giant clams and octopi.

Invertebrates make good subjects for projects and good additions to collections. They are easier to work with than vertebrates, and fewer restrictions apply to their use.

INSECTS

The most common invertebrates are insects. You will have no problem finding them. Millions of insect species compete with people for food, or on the other hand, help to provide that food. Weevils and beetles may infest stored flour, but bees pollinate blossoms, and without them there would be no apples, peaches, raspberries, or many other fruits. More needs to be learned about insects, so even a beginning observer and collector may discover new facts.

Insects live such short lives and are so numerous that in general you will do no harm by collecting and killing them. Exceptions are the large moths and butterflies, which have been over-collected.

Tools and Equipment

You will need some special but simple tools and equipment for collecting insects. These will include an insect net, insect pins, a killing jar, and pinning and spreading boards. You can buy these supplies at a biological supply house or hobby shop, but some you can make.

To make a net, follow the steps in Figure 11.

Insect pins come in special sizes and finishes, so you should buy them, not use sewing pins, which will rust. Get an assortment of sizes to fit different insects.

To make a killing jar to kill insects out in the field, mix ¼ cup (60 ml) of plaster of paris into an equal amount of water in a disposable container. Stir it until smooth, then pour into a pint-sized (500-ml), wide-top glass or plastic jar. Let the plaster harden.

Before you go collecting, drop in several cotton balls saturated with nail-polish remover. Cut a circle of stiff paper, punch a few small holes in it, and press it down on top of the cotton balls so insects will not become entangled in the cotton. See Figure 12.

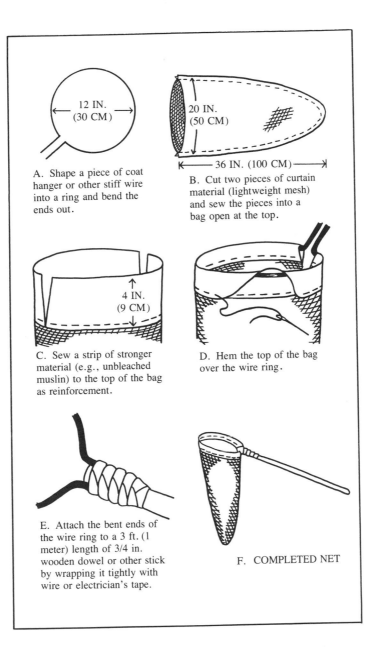

A. Shape a piece of coat hanger or other stiff wire into a ring and bend the ends out.

12 IN. (30 CM)

B. Cut two pieces of curtain material (lightweight mesh) and sew the pieces into a bag open at the top.

20 IN. (50 CM)

36 IN. (100 CM)

C. Sew a strip of stronger material (e.g., unbleached muslin) to the top of the bag as reinforcement.

4 IN. (9 CM)

D. Hem the top of the bag over the wire ring.

E. Attach the bent ends of the wire ring to a 3 ft. (1 meter) length of 3/4 in. wooden dowel or other stick by wrapping it tightly with wire or electrician's tape.

F. COMPLETED NET

Figure 11. Making an insect net

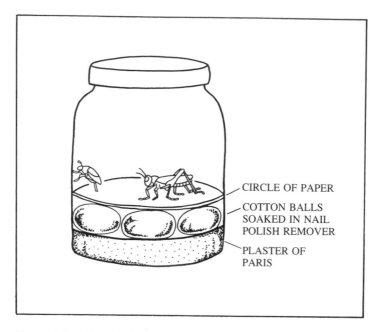

CIRCLE OF PAPER

COTTON BALLS
SOAKED IN NAIL
POLISH REMOVER

PLASTER OF
PARIS

Figure 12. A killing jar for insects

Collecting Insects

Look for insects in a variety of places: in the air, under bark, in rotten wood, under boards and rocks, on plants, under lights at night, in your house anywhere from cellar to attic, along lake and ocean beaches, in woods, fields, ponds, and streams.

Now, go hunting. You will find this a real challenge. Insects are swift fliers, but you may catch some on the wing with a deft sweep of your net. Flip the net over quickly to hold the insect in the base of the bag and carefully work the insect into the killing jar. Sometimes you can collect insects directly into the jar.

Replace the lid promptly after each use, to reduce evaporation. Leave the insects in the jar at least an hour, longer for beetles. When you come home, place the insects in jars and put the jars in the freezer for 24 hours to make sure the insects are truly dead.

If you are collecting near home, you can kill insects by placing them in covered jars in the freezer for 24 hours. This is a humane method, not unlike what happens to them in nature as winter comes on.

Collect just a few insects at a time, since you must mount or preserve them quickly before they stiffen and become unusable.

Field Notes and Labeling

Chasing insects is exciting, but be sure to take careful field notes. Record the date, locality, and weather conditions, like this: "10 July 1988. Michigan, Wayne County, Plymouth Township. 10:00 to 11:00 A.M. Sunny. Light breeze. 85°F." Then, for each insect or group of insects, record specific information: "No. 14. Flying over clover field." If you get more than one insect at one sweep, number them 14-1, 14-2, etc. Remember to keep the collection number with each specimen at all times.

Preserving Insects

You will need to preserve your insects quickly after bringing them home. Many can be preserved in rubbing alcohol, but do not use alcohol for hairy insects like bumblebees or scaly ones like butterflies and moths.

Many insects must be preserved by being pinned and spread. This requires a pinning surface, spreading board, and special insect pins.

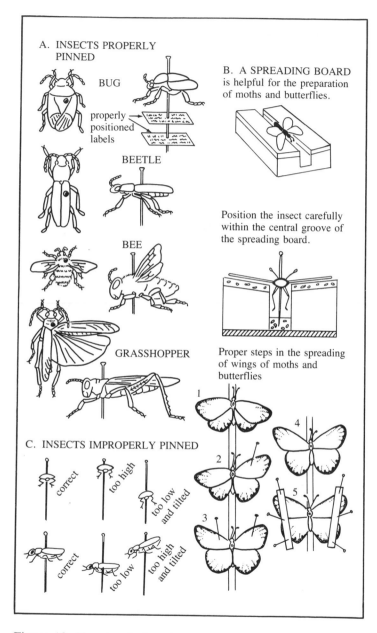

Figure 13. How to pin insects

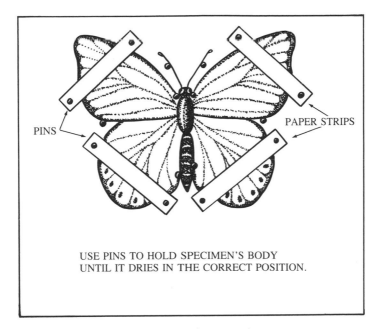

PINS

PAPER STRIPS

USE PINS TO HOLD SPECIMEN'S BODY
UNTIL IT DRIES IN THE CORRECT POSITION.

Figure 14. Spreading butterfly without pinning

Mount the insect by pinning it through the thorax as shown in Figure 13A. Leave space below it for labels. Arrange the legs and antennae neatly. Figure 13B shows how to pin a moth or butterfly, and Figure 13C shows the wrong way to pin insects.

Instead of pinning an insect through the body, you may simply want to spread and arrange the insect by placing pins around it and smooth strips of paper over it until it dries to the correct position. Refer to Figure 14.

A pinning surface may be as simple as a flat piece of insulation board, foam plastic, or corrugated cardboard, or it may be a box with a foam plastic bottom.

A spreading board is made of soft wood (balsa or bass-wood) or of other soft material into which pins slide easily. It has slanted sides and a groove for the insect's body, so that you can arrange legs and wings in uniform positions, not leave the insect all bent and twisted.

Identifying Insects

To identify your specimens and to learn the finer points of preservation, consult field guides to insects or some of the excellent 4-H or government publications. If you have preserved and labeled the insects carefully, they can be identified even years later.

INSECT RELATIVES

Spiders, daddy longlegs, sowbugs, centipedes, and millipedes are closely related to insects, and you will find them in the same places you find crawling insects. Figure 15 contains drawings of some of these creatures.

Capture these invertebrates in jars, and kill them at home by placing them in jars in a freezer for 24 hours. Preserve them in rubbing alcohol. Never pin any of these, although you might spread some on a flat surface to dry for special displays.

EGGS, WEBS, AND EXOSKELETONS OF INSECTS AND THEIR RELATIVES

Besides the actual insects or related creatures, you can collect "evidences," including eggs, webs, exoskeletons, and various traces (see Figure 16).

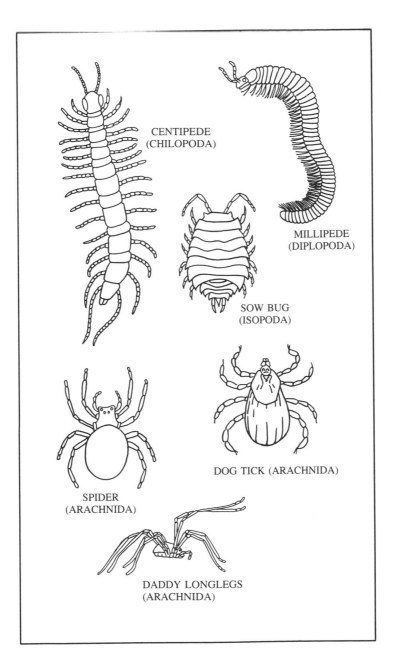

CENTIPEDE
(CHILOPODA)

MILLIPEDE
(DIPLOPODA)

SOW BUG
(ISOPODA)

DOG TICK (ARACHNIDA)

SPIDER
(ARACHNIDA)

DADDY LONGLEGS
(ARACHNIDA)

Figure 15. Insect relatives

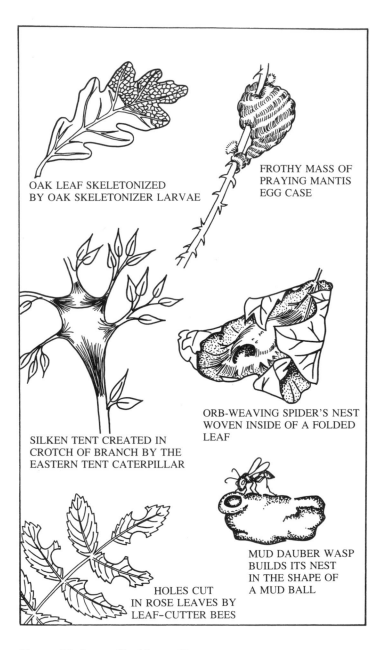

OAK LEAF SKELETONIZED
BY OAK SKELETONIZER LARVAE

FROTHY MASS OF
PRAYING MANTIS
EGG CASE

ORB-WEAVING SPIDER'S NEST
WOVEN INSIDE OF A FOLDED
LEAF

SILKEN TENT CREATED IN
CROTCH OF BRANCH BY THE
EASTERN TENT CATERPILLAR

MUD DAUBER WASP
BUILDS ITS NEST
IN THE SHAPE OF
A MUD BALL

HOLES CUT
IN ROSE LEAVES BY
LEAF–CUTTER BEES

Figure 16. Insect "evidences"

Look for eggs or egg cases on twigs or stems or on the undersides of leaves. Eggs may look like clusters of pinheads and are often brightly colored. Spider-egg cases sometimes resemble tiny smooth bags or cotton balls.

Also look for exoskeletons, discarded as insects grow, as well as the abandoned nests of mud or paper wasps. Look, too, for plants damaged by insects. For example, if you find a rose leaf with neat round holes, you are looking at the work of a leaf-cutter bee, which builds its nest from the circles. A leaf covered with squiggly lines is inhabited by a leaf miner, an insect so small it can live and eat between the two surfaces of the leaf!

Spider webs are also interesting to collect. To preserve a web, spray-paint it lightly with black or white paint. When it is dry, carefully sandwich it between two clean pieces of glass or plastic and bind the edges with clear tape. You can also photograph the web rather than collect it. Experiment with different backgrounds and try to find a web with a few beads of dew, for a more interesting photo.

RAISING INSECTS AND THEIR RELATIVES

You can also build a setup in which to observe the whole life cycle of an insect or similar invertebrate.

Collect some eggs along with the plant they are on, and place the plant in a jar of water inside a cage made of screen (see Figure 17) or in a glass jar with a screen top. Keep the environment in the cage at a tem-

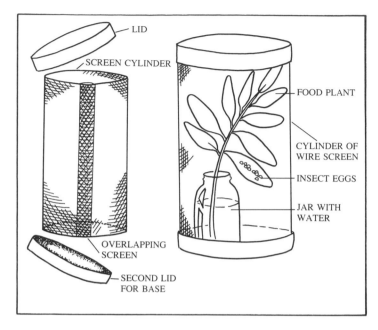

Figure 17. An invertebrate "farm"

perature and humidity similar to those where you found the specimen, perhaps in a garage or on a shaded windowsill, and wait. Eventually the eggs will hatch, and the young will feed and grow into adults. You can observe, record, photograph, and take samples of the different stages in the creature's life cycle. The result will be a fascinating display.

CRUSTACEANS

You are probably familiar with some of the invertebrates known as crustaceans: crabs, crayfish, lobsters, and shrimp. These hard-shelled creatures with seg-mented bodies and legs can be collected in watery places or bought in stores, and they make good additions to a collection of aquatic animals. Traces can be collected or documented without any killing—tracks, outgrown empty skeletons, lobster claws, and the shells of stranded bar-nacles.

If the shells or the claws are dry, store or exhibit them as they are. Otherwise, preserve them in rubbing alcohol.

MOLLUSKS

Mollusks are other invertebrates with shells. These in-clude snails, clams, mussels, oysters, and scallops. Col-lecting shells is fun, and nothing could be more fasci-nating than a colorful shell collection.

Land snails can be found in damp places, from home gardens to forests; water snails live in freshwater streams, ponds, and lakes, and in oceans, often clinging to plants. Shells of shellfish can be found on ocean and lake beaches; clamshells can also be found in some riv-ers. Be sure to put back any shellfish or snails whose shells are still inhabited, and avoid any rare mollusks. Although collecting empty shells is safe and legal at most beaches, look for signs anyway, and obey them.

Be careful when collecting at the seashore, es-pecially when you are at the foot of a cliff or climb-ing around on rocks at low tide. Go out at low tide, ideally when the tide is still going out, not coming in. A tidal chart (printed in newspapers) will tell you the times of the different tides.

Labeling Mollusks

Label specimens as you collect them and take field notes, paying special attention to location and color. Did you find the shell or creature underwater, on a rock, under wet sand 3 ft. (1 m) above the water line, or under dead leaves? Was the color bone white, pale pink, or dark gray? If you are serious about your mollusk collection, you will want to do some additional reading on the way that scientists classify the different zones of the beach.

Since labels are hard to attach to wet specimens, use labels on strings or put the specimens into labeled bags, cans, or bottles.

Preserving Mollusk Shells

To clean shells, gently wash and brush them. Store them dry, or, to emphasize their appearance when wet, store them in jars of mineral oil.

STARFISH, SEA URCHINS, AND SAND DOLLARS

Look for the skeletons of these creatures on ocean beaches, but do not collect living ones. Urchin skeletons need gentle cleaning to make them ready for display. All can be stored or displayed dry.

OTHER INVERTEBRATES

Tiny coral animals live together in vast colonies, secreting protective shells that build up over a long period to make whole ocean reefs or even islands. Watch for pieces

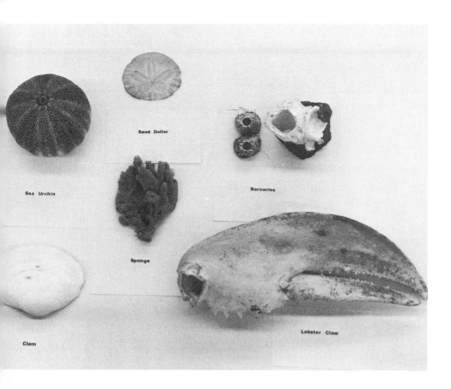

Seashore invertebrate treasures

of coral broken off and washed ashore after storms. You can also buy coral in stores.

Sponges are primitive animals that live in either fresh water or the sea, forming crusts on rocks and sticks. With luck you may find some sponges on an ocean beach. You can sometimes buy natural sponges at health-food stores.

Jellyfish are transparent, floating marine creatures that usually are impractical to collect. However, you might find the delicate, pale purple, sail-like fins of one species, the purple sailor.

Beware of other jellyfish. Some can deliver a severe sting.

Once you become familiar with some of the invertebrates described above, you can expand your search for some of the many other invertebrates, on both land and in water, that can be collected.

SIX

COLLECTING ROCKS, MINERALS, AND FOSSILS

Rocks and minerals are probably the easiest objects in nature to collect. There they are, everywhere underfoot, waiting. They are scientifically valuable, and they come in all colors and shapes, no two alike. They lend themselves to a great many kinds of projects, and they make fine displays.

Fossils—rocks embedded with the remains or imprints of organisms that lived millions of years ago—are much less common than rocks and minerals, but in certain areas they are fairly abundant. Finding a fossil such as the imprint of an ancient plant or fish is exciting, and fossils could turn out to be the most popular part of a nature collection (see Figure 18).

You can collect different kinds of rocks, minerals, and fossils, or you can collect specimens from different places. You can study unusual geological formations

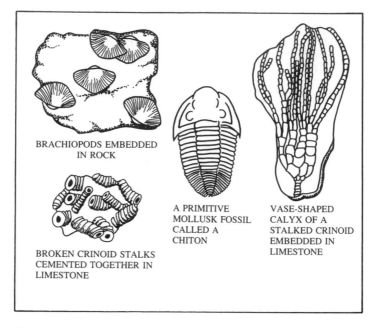

BRACHIOPODS EMBEDDED
IN ROCK

A PRIMITIVE
MOLLUSK FOSSIL
CALLED A
CHITON

VASE-SHAPED
CALYX OF A
STALKED CRINOID
EMBEDDED IN
LIMESTONE

BROKEN CRINOID STALKS
CEMENTED TOGETHER IN
LIMESTONE

Figure 18. Fossils

while collecting and model them—or display photos or sketches of them—next to the actual rocks. Minerals and semiprecious stones can be cut and polished with fairly inexpensive equipment called lapidary tools. Although you can buy samples of rocks and minerals, it is fun to collect your own, and your display will have much more meaning and involve more creativity.

Soils can also be collected, studied, and displayed. If you look at sand under a magnifying lens, you will find that it looks like a collection of tiny rocks or minerals. Can you find a way to separate out the different ingredients in a sand sample? What about collecting soil samples from different areas, from your backyard to the nearest mountaintop?

With rocks, minerals, and soils available almost anywhere, and fossils available in many places, you should have no trouble assembling a good collection that follows a plan of your own creation.

TOOLS AND SUPPLIES

You will need some special equipment: a geologist's or mason's hammer and a cold chisel for prying rocks loose or breaking them into smaller pieces; a sharp-pointed awl for delicate work; goggles to protect your eyes from flying rock chips; and pieces of newspaper for wrapping specimens. Take along your camera to photograph the site, or drawing materials to sketch it.

CAUTION: Keep a cork on the awl's point to protect yourself and the point when not in use, and be sure to wear the goggles when using any of the tools.

A FEW FACTS ABOUT
ROCKS AND MINERALS

Before you go into the field, you will need to know a few things about what you are collecting.

Rocks and minerals are not quite the same. All rocks are made up of minerals, but not all minerals are rocks. Salt, copper, sulfur, and oil are minerals. Think of them as substances found in rocks but having their own characteristics. Granite is a rock, made up of two or more minerals such as quartz and feldspar. Sometimes minerals occur in forms known as gems.

Rocks lying on the ground or beach are called *float*. Instead of being in their original position, they have been moved to that place by waves, glaciers, or people. Rock that lies beneath or crops up from beneath the ground and that is part of the earth's crust is called bedrock. Chips of rock lying at the base of a cliff, obviously broken off the rocks above, are called scree or talus.

WHERE TO COLLECT ROCKS AND MINERALS

You can collect on most public land unless signs warn against it. In state or national parks, forests, and monuments, be sure to check with a ranger on the rules there. If you want to collect on private property, obtain permission from the owner. Many quarries—places excavated for rock, minerals, sand, or gravel—allow collecting, but you will need permission.

If you are serious about your collecting, you will want to obtain a field guide to rocks and minerals. You can also use geologic maps, which you can obtain from your state geological survey or from a sporting-goods store. You may want to join a gem club. Another way to find good collecting sites is to keep your eyes open for rock shops, which are often located near sources of interesting rocks or minerals. Talk to the owners.

Rock collector
at work in winter

OBSERVE THE FOLLOWING PRECAUTIONS WHEN YOU COLLECT:

1. Try to go collecting with a knowledgeable adult. Always go with an adult when working near a highway, in a gravel pit or quarry, or where there is water.

2. Do not explore mine shafts.

3. Dig only in places where there is no danger of dislodging rocks that might fall on you, or of starting a landslide, or of your falling down a cliff.

4. Take a first-aid kit in case you cut yourself or bang your finger with the hammer.

5. Always tell an adult where you are going and when you expect to return.

Here are some places you might explore for specimens.

Beaches

Beaches are a good place to collect loose rocks and pebbles. Some beaches—for example, those along the coast of California above San Luis Obispo—have pebble beaches where semiprecious stones such as jade and jasper can be found. You can also collect vials of sand from different beaches or streambeds for a sand collection. Look also for sand along some trails and of course in the desert. How did it get there?

Highway Cuts

Highway construction often exposes interesting rocks and layers called strata that go back hundreds of millions of years in time. **Explore road cuts only under adult supervision.**

River Beds, Quarries, and Other Excavations

You can find bedrock in these places. A stream or river may have carried away all the soil in a place, or the process of quarrying rock or of digging a foundation may have exposed the bedrock. Unless it is exposed in a safely accessible place, however, you will need to ask the owner or a worker for samples, or be content with photos or drawings.

You may find pebbles, minerals, and fossils in streambeds and semiprecious stones such as garnet in a quarry.

Other Places

Many traces of glacial activity are evident throughout parts of the United States. Only an hour north of New York City, conglomerate rock (pebbles cemented together naturally) can be found with the pebbles neatly shorn by glacial activity. You can sometimes see the scratch marks of the ice. It is as if someone with a very sharp knife sliced off the tops of thousands of pebbles. In other parts of the country, boulder fields, or boulders strewn in a field, or a short rock ridge at the end of a valley may indicate that a glacier was once there. These are all good places to collect rocks that tell a story.

You can also collect right around your home, whether it is an apartment or a house. You might collect samples of different materials used in building. Don't, of course, start tearing out the foundation, but keep your eyes open for fieldstone or mine rock (from a foundation), slate (from a hallway or path), bricks and tiles made from clay, concrete (made of sand or gravel and cement), and glass (made of sand, lime, and soda). You may want to find out where each of the ingredients came from.

You can also obtain rocks at companies that manufacture portland cement or mortar (limestone), construction blocks (limestone or concrete), and tombstones (marble and granite).

WHERE TO
COLLECT FOSSILS

Fossils can be found in sandstone, shale, and limestone—rock originally formed from sediments that settled down, covered plants and animals, and finally became stone. Good places to look are in gravel pits, along lake shores, and in outcroppings of sedimentary bedrock in quarries, along streambeds, in gullies and canyons, in roadside cuts, and excavations of any kind.

Guide books, clubs, naturalists, highway engineers, and other collectors can direct you to any fossil digs in your area.

HOW TO COLLECT
ROCKS, MINERALS,
AND FOSSILS

Whatever you are collecting, you will want it to be of a manageable size. That means you may have to use your hammer and chisel to knock off a small piece from a large rock. A good size for a specimen is about 2 × 2 in. (5 × 5 cm) or smaller. Of course you won't want to break up gems or stones with an interesting appearance, or to break fossils. If you find a fossil that weighs 20 pounds (9 kg), either leave it where it is or come back for it with someone who can help you carry it.

Stick a square of tape on each specimen and write your collecting number on it. In your field notebook, include notes on whether a specimen is float, bedrock, or scree. Describe the condition of the rock or soil surrounding it. Was the whole layer of rock tilted? What does the rock above and below it look like?

Try to identify the specimen using a field guide, then wrap it in newspaper, tape the paper closed, write your field number again on the paper, and place it in your knapsack.

When collecting fossils, be careful not to break them. They are often very brittle. Protect them carefully when you carry them; if you break one, save the pieces and glue them together later.

When collecting soil samples, put each in a small vial or bag with a label. You might want to display soil samples along with pressed specimens of typical plants that grow in each kind of soil.

CLEANING SPECIMENS

When you bring home your rock and fossil samples, clean them by soaking, washing, and brushing them, being careful to keep their field numbers with or on them at all times. Wash gently at first, because some fossils are easily dissolved.

To make a permanent marker for your specimens, paint a ¾-in. (2-cm) circle or square on the back with white enamel. When the paint is dry, write the field number in the spot with waterproof ink. When the ink is dry, cover the number with clear nail polish or shellac.

If you need to trim away some of the rock, wear goggles and work on a heavily padded surface.

IDENTIFYING SPECIMENS

Although collecting and preserving rock and mineral samples is relatively easy, identifying them can be difficult, because often minerals with the same chemical composition look very different outwardly.

It is a good idea to find out from a book or expert the kinds of rocks and minerals you are likely to find where you are collecting. Then study the beginning chapters of a field guide to rocks and minerals and learn to carry out the tests—for hardness, color, crystal shape, and so on.

Identifying fossils is a little easier, and a good field guide may be all you need.

See page 80 in Chapter 7 for information on how to obtain help identifying specimens.

SEVEN

STORING, IDENTIFYING, LABELING AND CATALOGING SPECIMENS

Here you are with some specimens collected, cleaned, and preserved. More often than not, they will need to be stored for a while before you get them ready to display. Many of them need only to be kept from getting broken or dusty, but others require special protection. Also, they should be stored in an orderly way so that you can find them when you want them.

If you have not already done so, you will need to identify and label the specimens. You may want to collect some additional specimens to complete a display or project.

PROTECTION WHILE
IN STORAGE

1. Keep pressed plant specimens in their single sheets of folded newspaper, protected inside stiffer pa-

per folders. To kill any insects brought in with the plants, place them in a tightly closed plastic bag and put it in a freezer for two weeks. If this is not possible, fumigate them by placing several cotton balls soaked in nail-polish remover inside the bag. Store them in airtight containers such as metal or plastic boxes or tightly closed plastic bags, to protect them from mice, destructive insects, and mold. Add a few moth crystals to each container.

2. Store fumigated nests, fur, feathers, and other animal specimens in boxes with moth crystals.

3. Store bones, rocks, shells, and similar objects in compartmented boxes (to keep out the dust); egg cartons are useful for small specimens.

4. Store insects very carefully, since they can be damaged by mice and by other insects, as well as by mold. Some insects are so fragile their wings will fall off if touched.

Use sturdy, tight boxes or cases for spread or pinned insects. Cigar boxes or special insect boxes (from biological supply houses or hobby shops) are fine. See Figure 19. Cut a piece of plastic foam, insulation board, or even corrugated cardboard to container size and place it in the box bottom as a soft pinning surface. Fasten a mothball in one corner with insect pins, and if possible add a little bag of silica gel to absorb moisture. You can buy silica gel at florists, hobby shops, and scientific supply companies. Handle insects only with tweezers or forceps if possible, to avoid damaging them.

5. Since specimens stored in fluid may dry out, dip the container tops in melted paraffin (available at food markets) to make a tight seal. **Caution:** Melt par-

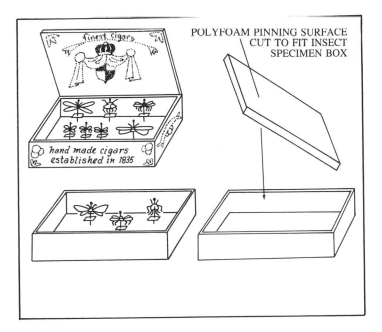

POLYFOAM PINNING SURFACE
CUT TO FIT INSECT
SPECIMEN BOX

finest cigars

*hand made cigars
established in 1835*

Figure 19. Insect storage boxes

affin wax in a container set in hot water, never directly
over a burner or flame, because paraffin can catch fire.

If you store your specimens by main groups—Plants,
Vertebrates, Invertebrates, and Rocks, Minerals, and
Fossils—you can find them more easily.

Remember to keep the field number on each specimen at all times.

STORING PHOTOS
AND OTHER ITEMS

Store photo slides in archival-quality (polyethylene or
Mylar) slide holders. Ordinary plastic will damage your

slides. Store prints and negatives in holders or albums made of the same archival materials or in envelopes made of special paper. Magnetic albums ruin prints. Use special boxes or files to organize your photos.

File pamphlets, cut-out pictures, charts, maps, letters, building plans, and other printed matter in alphabetized folders in a box or file cabinet.

IDENTIFYING AND CLASSIFYING

Some specimens are easy to identify, for example, a robin's nest, a dandelion, or a raccoon's track. Other specimens are harder, because there may be many similar species.

Most identification guides—whether for plants, animals, rocks, etc.—contain photographs, drawings, and text. Sometimes they have a key, a series of numbered choices that lead you to the correct name: "If there are clusters of five needles, turn to page 2; if there are clusters of three needles, turn to page 7." Read the instructions at the beginning of they key and follow the steps. Whenever you don't understand the meaning of a word, look it up in the glossary, a short dictionary of special words usually included in the book. Be patient and work carefully. At first you may think the key is impossible to use, but just keep trying. You will get better at it.

Most specimens have two names, a common name like "red clover," and a scientific name, *"Trifolium hybridum L."* Common names are unreliable, because different names may be used for the same species, or different species be called by the same name. Wild aster or Michaelmas daisy may refer to any of dozens of species of *Aster,* whereas the scientific name is the same in Kansas City or in Moscow.

Once you identify an organism or part of an organism, you may want to classify it by family, order, class, and so forth. For example, see how the deer mouse is classified in the chart on page 82.

For the most part, scientific names are Latin or Greek or a mixture of the two.

As you struggle to identify your specimens, you may only be able to place them in their family or even in their order. That is all right. Whatever you can determine, record it in your field notebook exactly as it was in the book. You may only be able to say, "Fly. Order Diptera," but if you have kept good records, someday you can identify it all the way to species and know which fly.

If you think you know what your specimen is, but you're not sure, write down the name and add a question mark. If you cannot make a positive identification, you will need to seek expert advice. Some people to try are teachers, 4-H or Scout leaders, geologists, naturalists, park rangers, hunters, farmers, and gardeners. If you still cannot find out what you have, write a museum, government agency (for example, the state geological survey), or the appropriate university science department. Write first, before you send them your specimen, enclosing a self-addressed, stamped envelope. If they are willing to help you, they will send shipping instructions. Always keep a duplicate specimen in case the one that is shipped gets lost, and be sure to include return postage. Many specimens, how-

CLASSIFICATION CHART

Scientists like to group organisms by their relation-
ships, starting with the largest group (kingdom) and
working down to the individual. Here are some sample
classifications. As scientists continue to study, some of
these may change.

Kingdom
  Division
    Class
      Order
        Family
          Genus
            species
              individual

Classification of the deer mouse (*Peromyscus manicu-
latus Wagner*):

Kingdom: Animalia (animals)
  Division: Vertebrata (animals with backbones)
    Class: Mammalia (mammals, animals that give
    milk)
      Order: Rodentia (rodents)
        Family: Cricetidae (mice and rats)
          Genus: *Peromyscus*
            species: *maniculatus*
              individual mouse

(*Note:* Wagner is the person who gave the deer mouse
this Latin name.)

ever, can be identified from field guides and by local advisors like teachers.

A specimen identified by an expert is a proud addition to your collection. You will name that person on the label as the identifier.

LABELING SPECIMENS

Your specimens should already be tagged with field numbers, and the numbers and descriptions listed in your field book, along with the identifications you have been able to put on them. Now it is time to talk about labeling.

In a collection made just for fun, a little card giving the common name, say, "Sugar Maple," is enough, but for a label of scientific value, the simplest one will contain at least the date and place of collection, neatly printed or typed on a 3×5-in. or smaller card. See Figure 20 for examples of good labels. The more information you can include on the label, the more valuable your specimen will be.

Photos and drawings can be labeled on the back and displayed with labels attached to the front or captions beneath them if hung on the wall.

Here are a few more suggestions on labeling:

1. For specimens mounted on sheets or cards, glue labels to the lower right-hand corner of the sheet.

2. For specimens stored in boxes, glue the label to the outside of the box.

3. For specimens preserved in fluid, print with waterproof ink on the smallest practical label and place

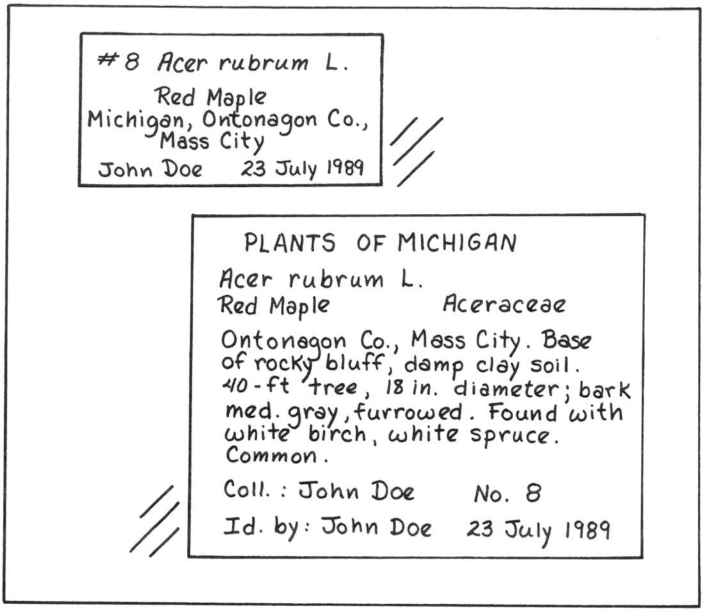

Figure 20. Examples of complete labels

it inside the vial or jar. Do not use ball-point or fiber-tipped pens. Pencil will make temporary labels in fluid.

4. Tie tags to antlers, horseshoe crabs, or claws.

5. For rocks or shells in trays, glue a small label in each compartment; or you can number the compartments and print a list with corresponding numbers and glue it to the inside of the lid.

6. Insects require small labels. Print the information with a very fine-tipped crow-quill pen, or a special lettering pen, using a magnifier if necessary. You can use two labels with pinned insects. The top label gives the place and date of collection and other information;

the bottom one gives the scientific name and your name and field number. Spread insects can have larger labels.

CATALOGING
AND ACCESSIONING

For most purposes, your specimens need be recorded only by their field numbers. If your aim is to build a professional collection, however, you may wish to learn cataloging (also called *accessioning*).

Your field number tells when you *collected* something; the catalog or accession number tells *when it was added to the collection,* after being properly processed. Most accessioned or cataloged specimens have been identified, but not all.

A simple cataloging system numbers by year and order of accessioning: 1988-1, 1988-2, 1988-3, 1989-1, 1989-2, 1989-3, and so on. If you already have a collection started before you start cataloging, simply begin with the present year.

Record your catalog either in a book with bound-in pages, or on 3 × 5-in. file cards, or in your computer (but be sure always to have an up-to-date printout). After the catalog number, copy all the field notebook data, including the field number and the name of the collector. Often you will have room for more information in the catalog than you can put on the label. Sometimes other people will give you things for your collection. Ask them to tell you the information about the specimen, and record it. Write in the common and scientific names, if known.

File cards are useful because you can make carbon

copies (or photocopies or duplicates on a computer) and make cross-files, grouped by collection locality, collector, or whatever category you like. The main catalog will be kept in order of catalog number. When your labels are 3×5 in., you can use copies of the labels for catalog cards.

Write the catalog number on each specimen and on its label. In the back of the catalog notebook or file, you might make a list of collection localities with complete descriptions, so that in other records such as your field notebook, you could just use an abbreviation, "our farm," "our yard," or "county park."

Cataloging takes time and effort but will add the final touch to your records. A good catalog will help you make your collection more of a museum than a simple display or assortment of specimens. A catalog can also help you organize the components of a science project built around a collection.

EIGHT

DISPLAYING
YOUR COLLECTION

So far, you have had the fun of hunting and collecting. You have carefully preserved your specimens and done the detective work of searching out their names. Now comes your chance to be really creative. In this chapter, you will learn how you can combine your specimens into displays that will tell stories and teach others what you have learned. A display could also be used as an exhibit in a more extensive collection (for example, one that could truly be called a museum), or for Scout, 4-H, classroom, or science fair projects. Even if your science project is not really based on a specimen collection, it will probably require a display.

A display can include specimens as well as posters, maps, charts, photos, drawings, pictures cut from magazines, and models.

TOOLS AND MATERIALS

The tools you may need include a hammer, saw, screwdriver, drill, ruler, square, box cutter or X-acto knife, scissors, paint brushes, crayons, pens, and felt markers.

You might set up a box marked "Display Materials" and begin assembling a variety of objects and materials helpful in making displays:

small boxes	plastic wrap
masking tape	tacks, nails
plaster of paris	waxed paper
plastic sheets	paraffin wax
pins	Mylar tape
paints	strong thread
modeling clay	cloth
plastic foam	wire
string	black enamel
colored paper	white glue

As you work you will discover more useful items.

DISPLAYS ON PAPER
SHEETS OR CARDBOARD

Mount lightweight, flat specimens on sheets of paper or cardboard.

Glue pressed plants to sheets of heavy, good quality paper. Sheets of special herbarium paper can be bought at biological supply places or college bookstores. If you decide to keep your collection in a three-ring notebook with pages $8\frac{1}{2} \times 11$ in., use watercolor paper or some other stiff paper. That marked "rag content" will last longer.

You will need white glue, a soft brush about ¾ in. (2 cm) wide, newspapers, waxed paper, corrugated cardboards about 12 × 18 in. (30 × 46 cm), and a damp cloth.

Paint the back of the plant gently with white glue slightly diluted with water. Pick up the plant with forceps or tweezers and lay it glue side down on the sheet, leaving room for a label in the lower right corner. (If the label is not yet ready, write your collection number on the sheet.) Blot away excess glue with a damp cloth, lay a sheet of waxed paper over the mounted plant, pad it with several thicknesses of newspaper, and lay it on a piece of corrugated cardboard. Set a heavy weight on top and leave it to dry for 24 hours. Of course, you can glue a series of plants in this same way, and pile them up, placing the weight on top of the whole pile. See Figure 21.

Glue stiffer plants, or twigs, to paper or cardboard. For extra strength, fasten narrow strips of cloth tape— if you can find it—across the bulkier parts. (Never use cellophane tape, which in time will discolor or become sticky.) You also can sew the plant on. Prick two little holes in the sheet, one on either side of the twig, run a piece of strong thread up and over, and tie the thread on the back of the sheet. Glue a square of paper over the knot to keep it from snagging on things such as other plants.

Wire coarse plants like cattail stalks to a piece of plywood or masonite with fine wire slipped through predrilled holes.

Glue, tape, or sew small bones or shells or any other very flat objects to cardboards. Standard poster

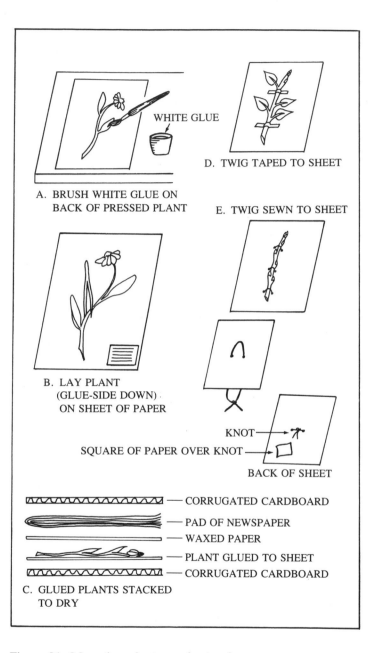

WHITE GLUE

A. BRUSH WHITE GLUE ON
   BACK OF PRESSED PLANT

D. TWIG TAPED TO SHEET

E. TWIG SEWN TO SHEET

B. LAY PLANT
   (GLUE-SIDE DOWN)
   ON SHEET OF PAPER

KNOT

SQUARE OF PAPER OVER KNOT

BACK OF SHEET

—— CORRUGATED CARDBOARD
—— PAD OF NEWSPAPER
—— WAXED PAPER
—— PLANT GLUED TO SHEET
—— CORRUGATED CARDBOARD

C. GLUED PLANTS STACKED
   TO DRY

Figure 21. Mounting plants on sheets of paper

board is a useful weight. It comes in sheets 22 × 28 in. (56 × 71 cm) and is sold at variety stores or art-material shops. Always leave room for labels.

Protecting Mounted
Specimens on Display

You can protect specimens on display with plastic protectors. Buy plastic-covered pages to fit a three-ring notebook, or use a photo album with plastic page covers, or spread plastic kitchen-wrap neatly over a specimen and tape the loose edges down on the back, or use a plastic bag. Clear contact paper works in the same way. You must be sure to position the contact paper correctly the first time, because you cannot take it off without ruining the specimen. Large Mylar envelopes (from a biological supply house) will cover a whole herbarium sheet.

Make a matched set of display envelopes by cutting a window in one face of a brown kraft paper envelope and slipping a plastic-covered specimen down inside. Leave a ¾-in. (2-cm) border around the edge. A set of tree leaves mounted this way looks very attractive.

Ordinary picture frames, especially the narrow black or metal ones, are excellent for displaying flat specimens under glass.

DISPLAYS IN BOXES

Specimens that are not flat, such as cones, fruits, bones, teeth, shells, or insects, should be stored and displayed in boxes.

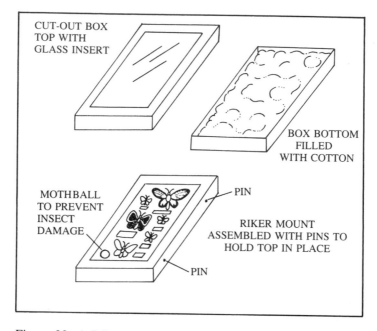

Figure 22. A Riker mount

The Riker mount (Figure 22) is one of the most useful display holders. It is a flattish box with a glass top, filled with cotton. You can buy various sizes from 2½×3 in. (6.3×7.6 cm) to 14×21 in. (36×53 cm) from biological supply houses or hobby shops, or you can make your own.

To make your own, use a flat box such as stationery comes in, about ¾ in. (2 cm) deep. With a box-cutting tool or X-acto knife, *carefully* cut away most of the lid, leaving a border about ½ to ¾ in. (1.25 to 2 cm) wide all around. Paint the box with black enamel.

When the box is dry, glue a piece of stiff clear plastic or of glass inside the lid, taping it in place as well. Lay a pad of cotton batting inside. Obtain cotton at a drugstore or quilt-supply store.

Arrange your specimens on the cotton. Include neat labels. Clean the glass or plastic well and set the lid in place. Hold the lid on with strong pins pushed in from the sides. For protection from insects, place a mothball inside, then cover all openings with tape. Shells and clean bones do not need moth protection, but insects and plants do.

You may display a whole exhibit inside one large Riker mount, or you may combine several smaller mounts into a larger exhibit.

For thicker specimens, use deeper boxes with glass tops. You can buy wood or cardboard boxes, or you can construct your own, perhaps from deeper stationery boxes or from those in which typing paper comes. You may fill them with cotton or not, depending upon the fragility of the specimens you are placing in them. Plans for a glass-topped wooden case are given in Figure 23. The insect storage containers you bought or built earlier can be modified to make display cases.

Boxes or trays with compartments are good for rock, mineral, and fossil specimens; for nuts, cones, and other fruits; and for objects in vials. Buy them or make your own dividers. Egg cartons can be painted to make neat display trays, and plastic kitchen wrap over the top will provide protection. Clear plastic boxes in a variety of sizes are sold in hobby, department, and office-supply stores. They make beautiful display cases.

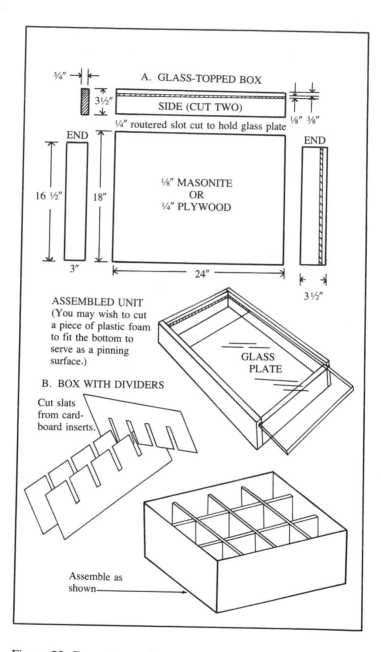

Figure 23. Deep storage boxes

Dioramas

A diorama is a special kind of display in a box or case that looks three-dimensional and very real. To make your own, use the drawings in Figure 24 as a guide. On the back wall of the box, draw or paint a picture of a suitable background, making distant objects such as trees or hills look smaller, and closer ones look larger. You could use a large photograph or cut-out picture there also.

On the floor of the box or case, place figures of animals, plants, or people. Twigs or weeds such as goldenrod can be used as trees. Those further back should seem to blend with the backdrop. When you visit a museum you will see exhibits set up this way.

Sometimes a diorama is placed inside a box with a hole for light in the top and a small peep hole at one end. When you look through the peephole the scene seems almost alive.

MODELS

You may want to incorporate models into your display. Models can be bought from supply companies and hobby shops, or you can make your own. To make your own modeling material, thoroughly mix one 16-ounce box of baking soda and 1 cup of cornstarch. Gradually add 1½ cups of cold water and cook the mixture slowly, stirring it constantly until it reaches the consistency of mashed potatoes. Turn it out on a plate. Keep it covered with a damp cloth.

When it is cool, shape the material like clay. Heat the oven to warm (200°F) and bake the figures slowly

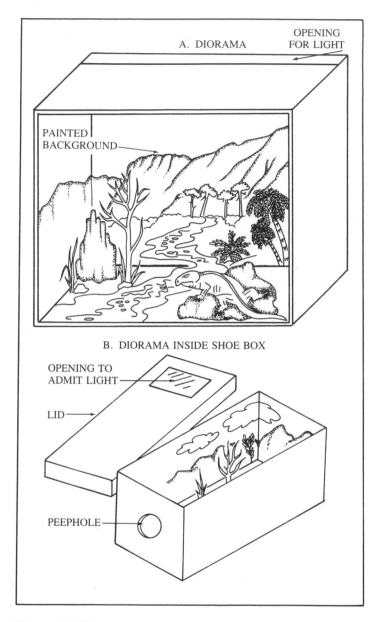

Figure 24. Dioramas

about an hour, a little more or a little less, depending on the size of the models. Turn off the oven and leave the figures in it all night.

Paint the models with watercolors, dry them thoroughly, then dip them in polyurethane varnish. These lasting figures are as fine-grained as clay.

BACKGROUNDS
AND BACKDROPS

Often you will need a background or backdrop for your exhibit. Backdrops can block out unwanted sights, or add color and interest, or provide a surface on which to pin or tape parts of your exhibit.

A School Showcase
To make a display inside a large glass showcase at your school, you might want to staple sheets of colored construction paper over the existing background. On that you can pin or tack up maps, charts, signs, specimens on sheets, and other lightweight objects. Attractive cloth instead of paper can be stretched over the background or over the floor of the exhibit. On the flat surface place heavier, three-dimensional objects such as skulls, models, or display boxes.

Freestanding Backdrops
Some freestanding backdrops can be built of a cardboard box or of plywood, pegboard, or insulating board or a combination of these. Keep in mind that you may have to transport it, and design it accordingly.

Figure 25. Cardboard-box backdrop

Cardboard-Box Backdrop

Cut away parts of a large cardboard box, leaving a back, floor, and parts of the sides as braces. Paint it with two coats of water-based paint to cover any lettering. This is lightweight, quite sturdy, and easy to carry. If you set the heavier objects on the floor of the box, you will make it more stable. Hang the lighter materials on the back and sides. See Figure 25.

Single-Board Backdrops

A single-board backdrop can have a prop fastened to its back or can be hung on a wall, as shown in Figure 26.

A good size is 3 × 4 ft. (90 × 120 cm). Pegboard has holes into which you can insert special hangers (from the hardware store), or you can use thread or wire to attach your specimens.

Plywood makes a sturdy backdrop. Fasten to it some foam plastic, insulation board, or even cloth for a good stapling or pinning surface.

For a county fair, one girl stretched sturdy cloth over a 3 × 4-ft. (90 × 120-cm) piece of plywood and tacked the cloth in place on the back. She glued pressed plants to cards and pinned the cards to the cloth. She collected plant seeds into vials and sewed the vials to

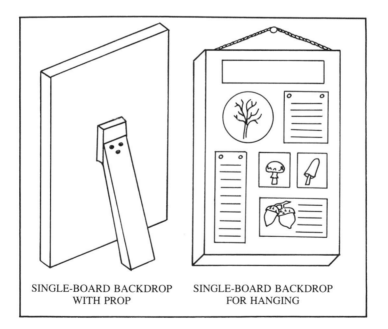

SINGLE-BOARD BACKDROP
WITH PROP

SINGLE-BOARD BACKDROP
FOR HANGING

Figure 26. Single-board backdrops

the cloth using elastic thread. She completed the display with labels, and her exhibit, "Ten Plants and Their Seeds," won a blue ribbon.

Three-Sided Backdrops
A hinged, three-sided backdrop is one of the most useful kinds. Build it well and you can use it over and over for different exhibits.

You could make it of cardboard or insulation board, gluing on cloth strips for hinges, as shown in Figure 27. Make it attractive with paint or with a cloth or paper covering.

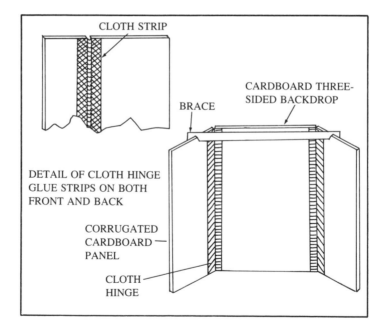

Figure 27. Three-sided backdrop of cardboard

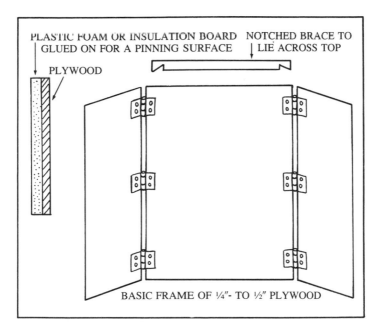

PLASTIC FOAM OR INSULATION BOARD   NOTCHED BRACE TO
GLUED ON FOR A PINNING SURFACE   LIE ACROSS TOP

PLYWOOD

BASIC FRAME OF ¼"- TO ½" PLYWOOD

Figure 28. Three-sided backdrop of plywood

You can build a backdrop of ¼-in. (.6 cm) to ½-in. (1.3 cm) plywood and glue insulation board or foam plastic to it for a pinning surface. Hinge the three pieces together with metal hinges, so it will fold flat when not in use. See Figure 28. Set it upright, lay a notched stick across the top for a brace to give it stability, and assemble your display upon and in front of it.

For your own collection, the whole wall can be a background. To use all the space, hang some things from the ceiling, or set up a freestanding exhibit. Imagine an actual branch of a shrub or tree set in a heavy container of sand, with your bird's-nest collection arranged among the twigs.

PUTTING TOGETHER
THE DISPLAY

As you assemble your displays, keep in mind several factors:

• Remember your central theme and arrange the objects to show that.

• Place larger, darker objects closer to the center or bottom, and smaller, lighter colored ones at the edges or top, for artistic balance. Heavier objects should be set down low, to keep your exhibit from falling over.

• Help visitors understand your exhibits with signs and information cards, but be brief. Let your specimens tell most of the story.

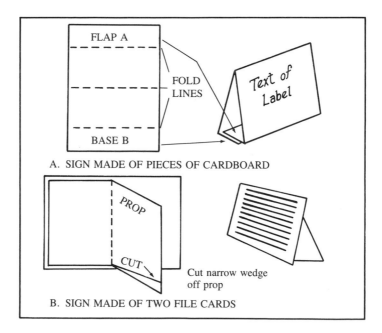

Figure 29. Making stand-up signs

Making Signs

Print or type signs neatly, using simple lettering. Use guidelines to keep the lines straight. Sometimes gluing a white card to a colored-paper background will draw attention. Some signs are tacked or stapled to the background, but if you need stand-up signs, here are two simple ways to make them, using 3 × 5-in. file cards or adapting the same method to larger pieces of cardboard.

Mark, score, and fold along measured lines as shown in Figure 29A at left. Fasten flap A to base B with glue or Mylar tape, thus making a little A-frame placard.

Or use two file cards. Print the sign on one. Fold the second one and glue or tape half of it to the lettered card. The second half makes a prop. If you cut a narrow wedge off the prop, so that the lettered card will slope a little, the sign will stand up better. See Figure 29B. You may make a small A-frame support for a larger card.

As you work with your materials, more ideas will come to you. Be imaginative and creative, use color and a variety of shapes and materials, and always work neatly and carefully so that your displays will inform and delight the observer.

NINE

PLANNING AND BUILDING A NATURE MUSEUM

This chapter is for readers who want to put a collection on display somewhere other than a science fair. You may already have one or more displays prepared. Or, you may want to begin by first setting aside space for your collection and then setting up shelves, cabinets, storage boxes, and so on. Your museum can be simple or elaborate, depending on your needs and resources and on how much time you have.

LOCATION

You will need a place for your museum. This could be at home, at school, at camp, or at a friend's or a relative's. You also will need a space—in a bedroom, garage, basement, attic, outbuilding, corner of your classroom, or wherever you can find room. If you are lucky, you might have a whole room. Otherwise you might use one wall or one corner of a room, or a closet.

Amy began her museum using one wall of her bedroom. In the summer she moved outdoors to an abandoned hunting shack on her family's farm, then in winter moved back indoors.

Mitchell's bedroom is in the basement. He set up one corner of his bedroom as a nature museum, with his prize-winning mounted porcupine skeleton as a focal point.

The students of Mr. Hoffman's class used the cases along one wall of the schoolroom to display a nature collection from the forest preserve and nature trail on the school grounds.

Evan lives in the city, so the theme of his museum, built on part of his bedroom wall, is "Wildlife in the City."

Jennifer's family operates a resort along Lake Michigan. She and a friend began with one case in the main chalet of the resort, then expanded to fill most of one wall. Resort guests enjoy looking at the exhibits and then trying to sight the living plants, birds, and animals in the surrounding forest and adding their own names to the list of bird sightings at the resort.

It would be nice to have a lot of space for your museum, as well as unlimited funds and time, but it's probably best to start small. One bookcase against your bedroom wall might be perfectly sufficient to display your small collection of rocks, shells, and feathers. If you enjoy that, you can expand.

If you have more specimens than you have room to display, don't be discouraged. Real museums display a small fraction of their holdings. Most of their collections are stored in boxes and cabinets in basements and other storage areas. You can store the bulk of your collection and display the best of it. You also can rotate your collection, changing the display from time to time.

THE PLAN

You will need a plan for your museum, to help you see it in your mind before you begin to move things around. You will want to know how much space you have, how much room the display units take up, and what you plan to display.

Begin by measuring the space—length, width, and height. Draw a plan to scale, letting 1 ft. be represented by 1 in. on paper. If you use the metric system, you can let 100 cm (1 m) be represented by 1 or 2 cm on paper. Using graph paper will make the drawing easier. Make two drawings, a floor plan as seen from above, and a view as seen from the front. The wall itself is part of your available space, because you can hang posters, pictures, and display cases on it. Figure 30 shows one possible design.

Make little cardboard cutouts, drawn to the same scale, of any shelves or other furniture you plan to use in your museum. Lay them on your floor plan and move them around, trying out different placements. You will be surprised to see how much you can arrange in the available space, and moving the cutouts is considerably easier than moving the furniture.

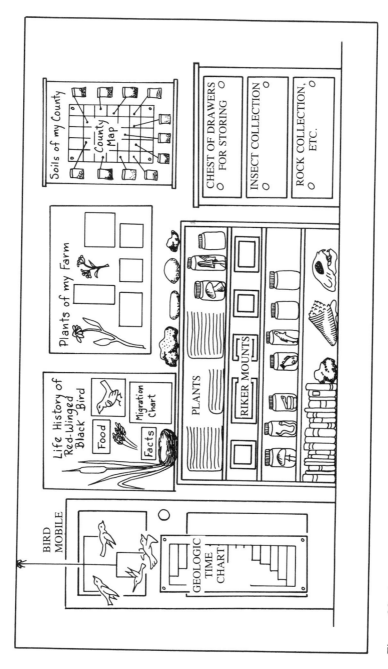

Figure 30. A museum on one bedroom wall

DISPLAY UNITS

You can utilize existing furniture or built-in shelving to display your collection, or you can build your own.

    • An easy way to utilize existing furniture is simply to display rocks, feathers, shells, bones, etc., on bookshelves. You can clear off a whole shelf or half a shelf, or you can even display objects in front of books. This is obviously not very fancy, but it beats keeping everything in boxes in the garage.

    • If and when you need more space, you can scrounge for or buy shelves or cabinets, or build your own. For some simple homemade units, make cardboard-box stackups or brick-and-board shelves. For the stackups, obtain six or eight sturdy cardboard boxes sized about $12 \times 12 \times 18$ in. (about $30 \times 30 \times 46$ cm). Carefully cut off the box flaps and paint the boxes with two coats of water-based paint to make them more attractive. Stack the boxes to make useful display shelves. See Figure 31. You can glue them together with white glue or leave them unglued. Heavier display objects can be put on the bottom shelves to make the exhibit more stable. For brick-and-board shelves, support a board on three piles of clean bricks or on cinder or concrete blocks, one pile at each end and one in the middle. Place something under the bottom bricks to protect the floor. To make another shelf, lay three more piles of bricks and another board. You can make about three shelves this way before risking the possibility that the shelves may fall over. You can paint the boards, but unfinished wood is attractive too. See Figure 32.

    • Other simple pile-up shelves can be made from wooden boxes or plastic crates.

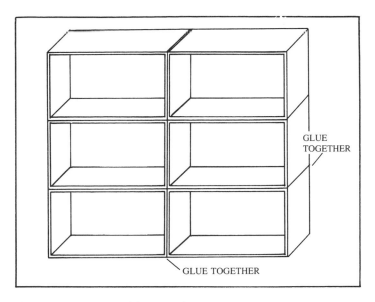

Figure 31. Cardboard-box stack-ups

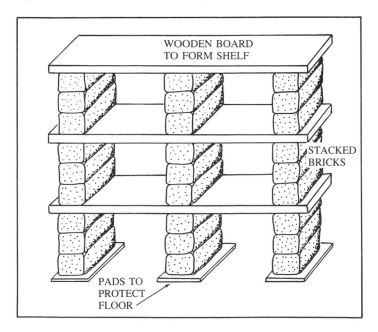

Figure 32. Brick-and-board shelves

• For more elaborate shelves, ask for help from your parents or your industrial arts teacher. If you are skillful at woodworking, study shelf plans in a good book on the subject. See the Bibliography. Mount shelves directly on the wall using brackets and special support strips, or build them of plywood.

• Cabinets with drawers are useful for storing specimens not in use at the moment, or for fragile insects. Professional insect cabinets have glass-topped drawers. You might find a good substitute in a used-furniture shop. Old music cabinets, china cabinets, and glass-fronted bookshelves are ideal for housing a small museum collection.

• If your museum occupies a whole room, placing shelf units back to back will increase the display space.

• Make a case that you can walk around, by constructing a glass-topped case and fastening it to the top of an old coffee table. Sometimes you can even obtain an old store showcase with glass top and sides, when a store is being remodeled or is going out of business. For a glass-topped case, use double-strength glass. Have the store cut it to the right size, and be sure the glass is supported at intervals for strength. Sheets of clear plastic from the hardware store will also make sturdy cases and may be even better for your purpose. For a larger glass-topped case, you can adapt the design shown in Figure 23. You will want to paint or finish your display shelves or cases. If you are working with wood, leaving the natural wood will make an attractive background for your collection. Sand the wood, stain it your favorite color, and cover with polyurethane or varnish, or else use regular paint. White is a good choice because nonwhite objects show up well. White or light-colored objects may be shown against dark backgrounds, perhaps in smaller cases or on boards.

Having set up these units, you now have somewhere to display the natural objects you have collected or which you intend to collect—your own nature museum. For more ideas for projects and displays, go on to the next chapter.

TEN

IDEAS FOR
DISPLAYS, EXHIBITS,
AND PROJECTS

In this chapter you will find a list of ideas for collections and projects utilizing new and existing specimens.

Plants

Algae: general collection, or from a particular place

Bark: samples, photos, or rubbings

Comparison of flower types or leaf shapes

Cones of different trees; male and female cones

Endangered or protected plants: drawings or photos

Enemies of different plants

Ferns and their relatives; fern families

Flowers: photos or pressed specimens from spring or
    summer

Flowering plants from a particular place—your yard or
    farm, a field, woods, pond, or vacant lot

Grasses: wild and cultivated

Lichens

Life cycle of one plant species

Life of (and in) a white pine or other tree

Mushrooms and other fungi; mushrooms and spore prints

Nuts and other fruit collections

Plant families: 10 or 12 different, or examples of one family

Plant galls and their insects

Plant uses: lumber, medicine, food, dyes, attracting wildlife

Poisonous plants: photos, cut-out pictures, or drawings

Seeds: collection; seed types; seed dispersal; sprouting

Trees: Collection or photos of flowers, leaves, and fruit of one tree or of different trees

Useful plants, such as wheat, corn, oats, and clover

Wild plants in the city

Wood samples: slabs or pieces of branches

Vertebrate Exhibits and Projects

Animal traces: bones, skulls, teeth, fur, horns and antlers, claws, and casts of tracks

Bird pellets from owls and hawks

Bird sightings you have made, illustrated with photos

Birds' eggs: models, photos, or drawings

Birds of a particular area: swamp, shore, meadow, woodland

Comparison of skulls, teeth, leg bones of different animals

Diorama of beaver dam, with models of animals

Display on one bird: feathers, photos, migration and range charts, nest

Fish scales, skeleton, fin types
Life history of one mammal, bird, fish, amphibian
Nests, abandoned
Photo essays on local wild animals
Photos of animals at night
Tape recordings of bird songs and calls; animal sounds
Wild animals of the city
Your pet as a wild animal: photos, tape recordings, notes
    on behavior

Invertebrate Exhibits
and Projects
Aquatic insects
Commercial uses of local marine invertebrates
Comparison of coral types
Effects of pollution on clams, mussels, etc.
Evidences of insects: egg cases, exoskeletons
Insect adaptation
Insect nests
Invertebrates in art
Life cycle of a cabbage butterfly or other insect
Life cycle of a marine invertebrate
Non-insect arthropods
Photos of invertebrates at the beach, in tidepools, etc.
Photos or drawings of shells
Photos or drawings of soft-bodied invertebrates
Seasonal study of black flies, deer flies, cluster flies
Shell collection: fresh-water, land, or marine
Spider webs
Termite life cycle
Useful and harmful insects

Rock, Mineral, and Fossil
Exhibits and Projects

Collection of rocks from one locality or area

Crystals and geodes

Crystal structure

Earth products in your home

Exhibit that shows effects of plate tectonics in your area (plate tectonics is one theory that explains the theory of continental drift and the formation of mountains and continents)

Fossil collection, keyed to maps

Fossil types

Geologic history of your area

Gifts of the glaciers: rocks left by, land forms, scratches on bedrock and boulders

How rocks form, with examples of igneous, sedimentary, and metamorphic rock, and geologic time charts

Photos of—and specimens from—unusual geologic formations, for example, obsidian or "black glass," pebble beaches, limestone caves, "cinder cones" (mounds of lava)

Photos or drawings of sand dunes at different times of day or year

Photos showing effects of earthquakes, faults, or other geologic action

Rocks from different places

Rock types

Soils: different types and composition

Soil types from your area

Uses of rocks

General Themes,
Interactions

Art objects with nature themes

Comparison of claws: crabs, spiders, insects, birds, and so forth

Diorama of how the area in which you live looked 350 million years ago

Diorama of how your area looked before Christopher Columbus

Ecology in your backyard: who lives on what?

Effects of acid rain on local vegetation

Exhibit on erosion

History of a famous local naturalist

Notebook: How you made your nature museum, with plans, drawings, photos, and a record of what you did

Plants used by local or ancestral Native Americans

Poisonous animals and insects of your state: photos, drawings, or cut-out pictures, and what to do if you encounter them

Postage stamps with nature themes

Samples from the seashore: crab claws and exoskeletons, fish bones, algae, driftwood, coral, sponges, starfish

Soil samples and typical plants from ten sites in your county, keyed to a map

What has been eating here? Plants partly eaten, gnawed nuts, snipped-off twigs, chewed bark, Twinkie wrappers?

Ideas for still more difficult science projects can be found in some of the books listed in the Bibliography.

BIBLIOGRAPHY

The following suggestions and list of books will offer you more information than could be given in this book.

As suggested earlier, look first for books and magazines written about the natural history of your own state or region. Because they do not describe all the insect species of the United States, for example, they will narrow the choices, making your work easier. To find such publications, ask your science teacher, librarian, or someone at the biology or geology departments of the nearest college or university, or write to your state department of natural resources.

Next, consult some of the well-illustrated series books. Check the Golden Guides, the Peterson and Audubon Field guides, the Pictured-Key Nature Series, Time-Life books, and National Geographic books. Dover Publications specializes in reprinting useful out-of-print books. Send for their catalog (31 E. 2nd Street, Mineola, NY 11501). Look for Boy Scout and Girl Scout manuals, and U.S. government and 4-H publications.

In the library, if you do not find exactly what you are looking for, search the card catalog under other related topics, such as Animals, Botany, Fish, Insects, Natural History, Nature, Plants, Seashore Life, Shells, or Spiders. Look at other books nearby on the library shelves. New books will give the latest facts, but often the older books include information that had to be left out of later ones because of space limitations. Look at both juvenile and adult books.

PLANTS

Gleason, H. A. *New Britton and Brown Illustrated Flora of the Northeastern United States and Adjacent Canada.* rev. ed., 3 vols. New York: Hafner, 1975.

Guberlet, Muriel Lewin. *Seaweeds at Ebb Tide.* Seattle: Univ. of Washington Press, 1967.

Hillson, Charles J. *Seaweeds: A Color-coded, Illustrated Guide to Common Marine Plants of the East Coast of the United States.* (Keystone Books) University Park, Pa.: Pennsylvania State Univ. Press, 1977.

Lawrence, George H. *An Introduction to Plant Taxonomy.* Toronto, Ontario: The Macmillan Company, 1955.

Lellinger, David B. *Field Manual of the Ferns and Fern Allies of the United States and Canada.* Washington, D.C.: Smithsonian Institution, 1985.

MacFarlane, Ruth B. (Alford). *Collecting and Preserving Plants for Science and Pleasure.* New York: Arco, 1985.

Muenscher, W. C. *Keys to Woody Plants,* 7th rev. ed. Ithaca, N.Y.: Comstock Publishing Associates, 1950.

Smith, Alexander H., and Nancy Weber. *The Mushroom Hunter's Field Guide: All Color and Enlarged.* Ann Arbor: The Univ. of Michigan Press, 1980.

Weber, Nancy S., and Alexander H. Smith. *Field Guide to Southern Mushrooms.* Ann Arbor: The Univ. of Michigan Press, 1985.

ANIMALS: VERTEBRATES

Goodson, Gar. *Fishes of the Atlantic Coast: Canada to Brazil, Including the Gulf of Mexico, Florida, Bermuda, the Bahamas, and the Caribbean.* CA: Stanford Univ. Press, 1976.

Hall, E. Raymond. *Mammals of North America,* 2nd ed., 2 vols. New York: John Wiley & Sons, Inc., 1981.

Hildebrand, Milton. *Anatomical Preparations*. Berkeley: Univ. of California Press, 1968.

Torres, John K. *The Audubon Society Encyclopedia of North American Birds*. New York: Alfred A. Knopf, 1980.

ANIMALS: INVERTEBRATES

Johnson, Sylvia A. *Crabs*. Minneapolis: Lerner Publications, 1982.

Pennak, Robert W. *Fresh-water Invertebrates of the United States*. New York: The Ronald Press Co., 1953.

ROCKS, MINERALS, AND FOSSILS

Daber, Rudolf, and Jochen Helms. *Fossils: The Oldest Treasures That Ever Lived*. Neptune City, N.J.: T. F. H. Publications, 1985.

GENERAL BOOKS

Brown, Vinson. *Building Your Own Nature Museum for Study and Pleasure*. New York: Arco, 1984.

————. *The Amateur Naturalist's Handbook*. Englewood Cliffs, N.J.: Prentice Hall, 1980.

Crosby, Alexander L. *Junior Science Book of Pond Life*. Easton, Md.: Garrard, 1964.

Gutnik, Martin J. *Ecology*. New York: Franklin Watts, 1984.

Haines, George. *The Young Photographer's Handbook*. New York: Arco, 1984.

Hussey, Lois J., and Catherine Pessino. *Collecting for the City Naturalist*. New York: Thomas Y. Crowell, 1975.

Knutson, Roger. *Flattened Fauna*. Berkeley, Calif.: Ten Speed Press, 1987.

Leslie, Clare W. *The Art of Field Sketching*. New York: Prentice Hall, 1984.

Saunders, John R. *Golden Book of Nature Crafts*. New York: Simon and Schuster, 1954.

Schuler, Stanley. *The Complete Book of Closets and Storage*. New York: M. Evans and Co., 1979.

Tocci, Salvatore. *How to Do a Science Fair Project*. New York: Franklin Watts, 1988.
Van Wormer, Joe. *How to Be a Wildlife Photographer*. New York: Lodestar Books, 1982.

MAGAZINES

Magazines are an excellent source of information. Once again, try to find some published for your own state or region. Sometimes libraries have to discard old magazines. Watch for these as a source of pictures, both to study and to cut out for displays.

Conservationist. 50 Wolf Road, Albany, NY 12233.
The Geographical Magazine. Geographical Press, Ltd., 1 Kensington Gore, London SW7 2AR.
National Geographic Magazine. National Geographic Society, Washington, DC 20036.
National Geographic World. National Geographic Society, Washington, DC 20036.
National Wildlife and *International Wildlife*. National Wildlife Federation, 8925 Leesburg Pike, Vienna, VA 22184.
Natural History. The American Museum of Natural History, Central Park West at 79th Street, New York, NY 10024.
Nature Canada. Canadian Nature Federation, 453 Sussex Drive, Ottawa, Ontario K1N 6Z4.
Oceans. Oceans Magazine Ltd. Partnership, 2001 W. Main Street, Stamford, CT 06902.
Oceanus. Woods Hole Oceanographic Institution, 93 Water Street, Woods Hole, MA 02543.
Odyssey. Astro Media, Kalmbach Publishing Co., 1027 N. 7th Street, Milwaukee, WI 53233.
Owl, The Discovery Magazine for Children. P.O. Box 11314, Des Moines, IA 50340.
Ranger Rick. National Wildlife Federation, 8925 Leesburg Pike, Vienna, VA 22184.
Scienceland. 501 Fifth Avenue, New York, NY 10017-6165.
Sea Frontiers. International Oceanographic Foundation, 3979 Rickenbacker Causeway, Virginia Key, Miami, FL 33149.

Smithsonian. The Smithsonian Institution, 1000 Jefferson Drive SW, Washington, DC 20560.

Weatherwise. Helen Dwight Reid Educational Foundation in Association with American Meteorological Society, 4000 Albemarle St., NW, Washington, DC 21116.

Wilderness. The Wilderness Society, 1400 "Eye" St., NW, Washington, DC 20005.

Your Big Backyard. National Wildlife Federation, 8925 Leesburg Pike, Vienna, VA 22180.

SCIENTIFIC
SUPPLY COMPANIES

Carolina Biological Supply Co.
Burlington, NC 27215
or, Powell Laboratories Division
Gladstone, OR 97027

Connecticut Valley Biological Supply Co.
Valley Road
Southampton, MA 01073

Edmund Scientific Co.
101 E. Gloucester Pike
Barrington, NJ 08007

General Biological Supply House
8200 S. Hoyne Avenue
Chicago, IL 60620

SKULLduggery, Inc. (skull and skeleton models)
621 S. "B" Street
Tustin, CA 92680

Wards Natural Science Establishment
P. O. Box 1712
Rochester, NY 14603
or, P. O. Box 1749
Monterey, CA 93940 .

Young Naturalist Catalog
614 E. 5th Street
Newton, KS 67114

INDEX

Rubbings, use of, 19, 26, *26*

Safety precautions, 21–22, 48, 63, 66, 69, 72, 73, 76, 78–79
Sand dollars, 64
School science projects, 9, 10
School showcase displays, 97
Science fair projects, 9, 14–15, 37
Scientific experimentation, use of vertebrates in, 37
Scientific names, 80–81
Scouts science projects, 9
Scree, 71, 75
Sea urchins, 64
Semiprecious stones, 72, 73
Sewing specimens for display, 89
Shell collecting, 10, 51, 63, 114
Shelves, display, 108–110
Signs, display, *101,* 103
Single-board backdrop, 98, *98*
Skeletons, collecting, 40, *41, 42, 43*
Skins and hides, preserving, 50
Snake skins, collecting, 43
Soft-bodied invertebrates, 51
Sponges, 65
Starfish, 64
State extension services, 23
Storage boxes, *94*
construction of, 78
Storage of specimens, 48, 77–80
Stuffed animals, 10

Summer camp science projects, 9

Talus, 71
Tape recordings of animal sounds, 46–47, 114
Taping specimens for display, 89
Taxidermy, 37, 50
Techniques of collecting, 13–23
Three-sided backdrop, *99,* 100, *100,* 101
Tidal chart, 63
Tools and supplies used in collecting, 15, 52, 69
display materials, 88
Tracks, animal, 10
making casts of, 43, 49, *49*
Trapping vertebrates, 37–38

United States Department of Agriculture, 22

Vertebrates:
collecting, 36–47
preserving, 48–50
suggested displays, 113–114

Water snails, 63
Webs, insect, 58, 61, 114
Wiring specimens for display, 89
Wood samples, 26–27, 35, *35,* 113
Woodworking, 110